Welcome Baby

A GUIDE TO THE FIRST SIX WEEKS

Anne Marie Mueser, Ed.D.
George E. Verrilli, M.D., F.A.C.O.G.

ST. MARTIN'S PRESS / NEW YORK

Library of Congress Cataloging in Publication Data

Mueser, Anne Marie

    Welcome Baby. A Companion Volume to the Authors' While Waiting
      1. Infant (Newborn) Care.

I. Verrilli, George E.   II. Title.

RJ253.M83   649'.122   81-16696

ISBN 0-312-86121-4   AACR2

Manufactured in the United States of America

Editor: Barbara Anderson
Design and Typesetting: Barbara Sturman; *Production:* Harry Chester Associates
Illustrations: John Frost and Annie Mueser

ACKNOWLEDGMENTS

Successful delivery of a book (as well as a baby) often depends on the support of others. The authors would especially like to thank:

—the administration and staff at Northern Dutchess Hospital, for providing a supportive atmosphere for family-centered childbirth and setting for our work

—the many mothers who were willing to be interviewed, and the nurses who helped, especially Bea A'Brial and Elaine Wood

—Barbara Sturman, who designed pages and set type with amazing speed and accuracy, and provided welcome support throughout the production process

—Harry Chester and his staff, who once again took our bits and pieces and made them into a beautiful book

—Dr. Abraham Nussbaum for consultation on the A to Z reference section of WELCOME BABY, and his helpful suggestions

—Dr. Lynne Liptay for her review of the manuscript, thoughtful suggestions, and encouragement on busy days

—Hospital Portrait Service for permission to use the cover picture, and Hal Abrams of Frenchy's Color Lab for printing it so well before the deadline

—Bert Lummus for sending us to St. Martin's Press

—our editor, Barbara Anderson, whose suggestions and encouragement were very welcome

—and perhaps most of all, Ánna Máire and her daddy, without whom there would be no book.

TABLE OF CONTENTS

ABOUT THE AUTHORS

Anne Marie Mueser, a writer and teacher for more than 15 years, has worked in elementary schools as a classroom teacher and reading specialist, and in clinical settings with learning disabled and dyslexic children. Formerly an Associate Professor of Education at Teachers College Columbia University, Dr. Mueser left the university in 1978 to devote her professional energies to her career as a writer. She is the author of numerous children's books and educational materials, and is presently working on a novel.

Her first child, Ánna Máire, was born in August of 1980, and Dr. Mueser now enjoys combining motherhood with her work as a writer. She and her daughter divide their time between their home in Dutchess County, New York, and County Galway, Ireland.

George Verrilli, a practicing obstetrician for more than 20 years, has delivered more than 6,000 babies. He received his M.D. degree from the University of Turin, and is a Fellow of the American College of Obstetricians and Gynecologists.

Dr. Verrilli is Chief of Obstetrics and Gynecology at Northern Dutchess Hospital in Rhinebeck, New York, where he has been a member of the hospital's Board of Directors since 1968. Under Dr. Verrilli's leadership, the obstetrical service at Northern Dutchess pioneered in implementing family-centered childbirth practices in a hospital setting.

Dr. Verrilli is married and the father of three sons.

ON THE COVER

Ánna Máire Mueser—delivered by Dr. Verrilli— arrived on August 13, 1980, at 3:07 p.m. She weighed 6 pounds 6 ounces and was 18 inches in length. The cover picture was taken a day later by a member of the Mothers' Club of Northern Dutchess Hospital, under contract with Hospital Portrait Service.

Note the shape of Ánna Máire's head, the slightly swollen eyelids, the wrinkled skin on her hands, and the way one hand is curled into a little fist. These are all typical characteristics of a newborn. The picture on the back cover of **Welcome Baby** was taken when Ánna Máire was ten months of age.

INTRODUCTION

Welcome Baby: A Guide to the First Six Weeks, contains many things I wish I had known a year ago, when my daughter Ánna Máire was born. The joy of the first moment I held her in my arms was quickly joined by the realization that I had a lot to learn. Much of the early research for **Welcome Baby** was done in self-defense! Fortunately for both mother and child, my friend Dr. Verrilli is a physician whose support and concern do not cease when the baby is delivered and the birth certificate signed. This volume is a result of our joint efforts and my learning experiences as a new mother, along with advice and encouragement from a number of mothers who gave birth at Northern Dutchess Hospital, and the attending pediatricians and nursery staff there.

Common sense is one of the most important ingredients of caring for a child. Don't be afraid to follow your own instincts, particularly when you have information to back them up. We hope that **Welcome Baby** will provide some of the information you need. Use this material as you work with your baby's pediatrician, who may help you modify some of the suggestions if necessary for your baby.

You'll notice that unlike some other baby care books, we don't have a special section addressed to the baby's father. This is deliberate. All the suggestions for taking care of your new baby (with the obvious exception of breast-feeding) are intended for *both* parents. We hope you'll share the pleasures and tasks of parenting in whatever ways suit you best.

Anne Mueser

Anne Marie Mueser, Ed.D.

Publisher's Note

The suggestions, procedures, and other materials in this book are not intended as a substitute for consultation with your physician. Medical supervision is recommended for care of your new baby and any other matters concerning your family's health.

This book belongs to:

Doctor's Name:

Address:

Telephone:

Hospital:

Address:

Telephone:

Emergency Numbers:

SECTION ONE

WELCOMING YOUR BABY

Getting Ready / Welcoming Your Baby / Leboyer Delivery /
Bonding (Bonding and Hospital Policies, Ingredients of
Bonding, Nursing Right After Delivery, Bonding as a
Continuous Process) / Characteristics of a Newborn (What a
Newborn Looks Like, Reflexes of a Newborn) / What Is
Done for Your Baby? (Identification, Apgar Rating, Additional
Medical Procedures, Care of the Mother After Delivery) /
Premature Babies / Circumcision: Yes or No? (Reasons For
Circumcision, Reasons Against Circumcision) / Naming Your
Baby (First and Middle Names, Last Names, Birth Certificate) /
The First Few Days at Home (What to Do, Other People,
"The Blues") / Choosing a Pediatrician (Finding
Pediatricians, Meeting the Doctor)

GETTING READY

During the last few weeks of pregnancy, many women experience moments of wondering if the baby will ever arrive. Pregnancy, at times, seems to be an almost eternal condition. Feelings like these often alternate with the opposite extreme—worry that there's so much to be done and so little time.

> For a concise guide to prenatal care, see **While Waiting: A Prenatal Guidebook,** by George E. Verrilli, M.D. and Anne Marie Mueser, Ed.D. (St. Martin's Press, New York: 1987). This companion volume to **Welcome Baby** provides information on pregnancy, labor and delivery, and postpartum care in a format designed for easy reference.

If your baby is due to arrive shortly, you've probably already made a number of important decisions about your care and the care of your new baby. If you've worked closely with your obstetrician, you may already have become familiar with some of the procedures he or she routinely uses and the policies of the hospital where you expect to have your baby. Perhaps you have already completed childbirth preparation classes to help you get ready for labor and delivery. You may already have visited the hospital where you plan to give birth.

Probably the greatest portion of the preparation efforts while you are pregnant will be focused on getting you and your partner ready for delivery. Most childbirth preparation classes give you the information you need to participate in the process of getting your baby into this world. But then what? The next few pages of **Welcome Baby** are designed to help you get ready for the moment of your baby's arrival and begin coping with the new experiences that follow.

WELCOMING YOUR BABY

How do you plan to welcome your baby? Most childbirth preparation classes focus on techniques for a mother to give birth with a minimum of fear or pain. Far less attention, if any, is given to what will be done to and for the baby during delivery. Part of your personal preparation should include careful consideration in advance of the atmosphere in which your child will enter the world. Discuss these matters with your obstetrician well before your baby is due.

> For an in-depth discussion of pregnancy and childbirth, one of the best works currently available is **The Complete Book of Pregnancy and Childbirth**, by Sheila Kitzinger (Alfred A. Knopf, New York: 1980). The material is sensitively written and beautifully presented, with numerous photographs and drawings.

No one else's words—perhaps not even your own—can adequately describe what your feelings will be at the moment your baby is born. Seeing and holding your newborn for the first time will be an occasion unlike any other, and this is likely to be so even if you have other children. Each baby is unique, and the experience of his or her arrival is a very special event. No matter how long, or how difficult the labor has been, the presence of your new baby will immediately help you put out of your mind any of the pains or discomforts you might have experienced while giving birth.

LEBOYER DELIVERY

Many hospitals now permit (or even encourage) the use of the gentle birth procedures developed by Frederick Leboyer, a French obstetrician. In an effort to minimize trauma to the newborn at birth, Leboyer keeps the environment as tranquil as possible, with dim lights and little noise. A warm bath shortly after delivery is designed to help the baby make the transition from the mother's fluid-filled womb to the world outside. The Leboyer bath provides an excellent opportunity for the baby's father to participate in bonding and caring for the new arrival. This approach involves greeting a baby with kindness and courtesy, and the philosophy can be incorporated into your birthing experience even if you are unable to or choose not to follow all the specific procedures Leboyer prescribes.

> To find out more about gentle birth, read **Birth Without Violence**, by Frederick Leboyer (Alfred A. Knopf, New York: 1975). This book is beautifully written and illustrated with photographs, and it's worth reading even if you disagree with some the details of Leboyer's philosophy.

BONDING

What is bonding? When does it begin? Bonding is the process by which parents form a close connection with their new baby beginning right after the baby's birth. The time immediately following delivery is now recognized to be very significant in the development of a relationship between mother and infant, and between father and infant as well, if the father is able to be present.

BONDING AND HOSPITAL POLICIES

In the past, the policies of most hospitals focused on the efficient medical processing of a mother and her newborn. The infant was (perhaps) briefly shown to the mother and then examined, washed, wrapped, and sent—not unlike a package—to the nursery to be clinically observed. The mother's body was repaired as needed, and then wheeled to another room where the woman could "recover" from her "ordeal." The baby's father, who had been kept at a distance (out of the way) from all these proceedings, was informed of the new arrival.

Now, however, more and more hospitals are permitting family-centered childbirth in which both parents can actively participate. Parents are encouraged to enjoy the contact with their new baby right after the baby is born. Bonding— the development of a feeling of belonging—is the beginning of a lifelong process of communication between and among family members.

Well before your baby is due, it's a good idea to discuss with your doctor what opportunity you will have to be with your baby immediately after delivery. Make your expectations known, so that your medical team is aware of what you think will contribute to making the birth experience meaningful for the entire family. Don't assume that every hospital will be organized to facilitate exactly what you wish. Some are more consumer-oriented than others. If what you want is medically safe, but unavailable to you with your doctor or hospital, you might consider making a change. Communication in advance is definitely preferable to disappointment later.

INGREDIENTS OF BONDING

• The time immediately after birth is optimum for you to get to know your baby and for your baby to get to know you. Both parents should be encouraged to share this time with their baby and an uninterrupted period of time should be provided so they can do this.

• Direct skin-to-skin contact between mother and baby is desirable. The baby can be placed on the mother's abdomen while the placenta is being delivered and during any repair work that follows. A blanket over both will help keep the baby warm.

• Eye contact between parents and baby is important. A delay in administering the required silver nitrate drops will insure that this initial contact is not hindered.

• Both parents should touch and talk to their baby.

• Immediate nursing of a newborn contributes to the bonding process.

NURSING RIGHT AFTER DELIVERY

The best time to begin breast-feeding is as soon as possible after your baby is born, if there haven't been any complications during delivery. Immediate nursing is best for both mother and baby. Nursing stimulates the uterus to contract and helps it return to its normal size more quickly. Many babies have an instinctive sucking reflex that is quite strong right after birth. If not stimulated right away (within an hour or so), this reflex may diminish somewhat for a day or two. Early nursing strengthens the bonding between mother and child. Some babies, however, don't seem to be especially interested in nursing immediately after birth. If this is true of your baby, don't be concerned or feel rejected. Use this time to cuddle and enjoy holding your baby.

BONDING AS A CONTINUING PROCESS

Although the term *bonding* is often used to refer to what is happening between parent and child immediately after birth, the process of developing a relationship with your new baby does not end in the delivery room. Bonding begins right after the baby's birth, but the process keeps going on as the parents and baby continue to interact.

Developing feelings of belonging is a gradual, long-term process. Sometimes—as in cases of complications during delivery, an infant at risk, or an inflexible hospital policy—it is impossible for parents and infants to bond immediately. Although the period immediately after a baby's birth is an extremely sensitive time for bonding to begin, if for some reason this time is not available to you and your baby, do not become discouraged. Begin bonding as soon as you are able. You have not failed; you've just started later.

CHARACTERISTICS OF A NEWBORN

When your first baby is born, you're likely to be surprised at what he or she actually looks like moments after birth. Even if you have other children, you've probably forgotten just how tiny a newborn can be.

First-time parents who expect that their newborn will approximate the appearance of infants pictured on baby food jars or diaper boxes may be somewhat shocked and disappointed when they see their new arrival. The cheerful, round-faced infants in the ads are usually several months old. Newborns just don't look like that.

WHAT A NEWBORN LOOKS LIKE

Your new baby is likely to have wrinkled skin, a lumpy head, and puffy eyes. He or she may still be coated with vernix caseosa (the protective covering that aids passage through the birth canal). The skin of some newborns is covered with lanugo (fine dark hair which will disappear completely within a few months).

A newborn baby's head seems to be disproportionately large for the rest of the body. For a full-term baby, the head is about one-fourth of the entire body length, and the circumference of the head is about the same as that of the chest. The shape of the baby's head—which has just molded to pass through the birth canal—may seem a bit odd. Some babies are born with a large squashy lump on the head, where the head was pressing down through the partially dilated cervix. This swelling, called a caput, will gradually disappear and is no cause for concern. There are two soft spots (fontanels) on a baby's head. These permitted the head to mold and fit through the birth canal.

The neck of a newborn often seems to be very short, and many babies have receding chinlines, bruised or crooked ears, and flattened noses. These features straighten out with time.

The genitals of a newborn of either sex may appear to be swollen. Both boys and girls may have swollen breasts with a bit of milk. (This is a result of hormone change after delivery, and it will stop without treatment.) Some baby girls also show some vaginal bleeding. This too will stop within a few days.

A newborn baby's hands and feet may appear somewhat bluish. The legs, which have been curled up inside the mother's body, look crooked. Some babies have patches of slate-blue coloring on the back, buttocks, or abdomen. These birthmarks, called Mongolian spots, usually fade within the first year.

REFLEXES OF A NEWBORN

At birth, a baby has a number of reflexes which help in the adjustment to living on his or her own. Among these are:

• *Sucking Reflex.*   When the lips are touched, the baby sucks. Touching the roof of the baby's mouth intensifies the sucking reflex.

• *Rooting Reflex.*   When you touch the side of a baby's face, he or she will turn in that direction and open the mouth to suck.

• *Moro (Startle) Reflex.*   If the baby hears a sudden loud noise, or is handled roughly, he or she may startle and throw both arms.

• *Grasp Reflex.*   Offer a finger or similar object, and the baby will usually grasp it and hold on tight.

WHAT IS DONE FOR YOUR BABY?

As soon as a baby is born, he or she must make the transition from being totally dependent on the mother, to functioning on his or her own. The birth attendants assist the newborn, as needed, in making this transition. If the baby is in respiratory distress, helping him or her to breathe is a top priority. Mucus is suctioned from the baby's mouth, if necessary. Because the room temperature is significantly lower than the mother's body temperature (which the infant has been used to until delivery), the baby must be kept warm. For warmth, the baby may be placed on the mother's abdomen and a blanket used to cover them both.

To complete the baby's passage to life outside the mother, the cord must be cut. While some doctors prefer clamping and cutting the cord immediately after the baby is delivered, many choose to wait until the cord has stopped pulsating before cutting it, unless there is some specific medical indication for doing this sooner in a particular case.

IDENTIFICATION

Before mother and baby leave the delivery room, they receive matching identification bracelets to ensure that no baby is ever given to the wrong mother. Many hospitals place two bracelets on the baby—one on an ankle and one on a wrist—as an extra safeguard. Each time a baby is brought to the mother, the identification is checked. As part of the permanent birth record, the baby's footprints may be recorded along with the mother's thumbprints.

APGAR RATING

The baby's condition at birth is observed and rated in five areas on a scale of 0 to 2. This rating, known as the Apgar Scale, is repeated when the baby is five minutes old.

Apgar Scale

Item Tested	0	1 point	2 points
Heart Rate	absent	slow (less than 100 beats per minute)	100 beats or more per minute
Breathing	absent	slow or irregular	regular
Muscle Tone	limp	some motion of extremities	active motion
Skin Color	blue	pink body, blue extremities	pink all over
Reflex Response	absent	grimace	cry

A score of 7 or above indicates that the baby is in good condition. Most babies score 7 or more by the five-minute check. For a baby who scores 4 or less, immediate intervention is required.

The Apgar Scale, named for Dr. Virginia Apgar, the physician who developed it, is a useful device to assess a baby's condition right after birth. It is not, however, a predictor of long-term health, but simply an indication of how well a baby has come through the stress of delivery.

ADDITIONAL MEDICAL PROCEDURES

In most states, babies are required by law to receive eye drops of a silver nitrate solution to prevent infection. Because the drops may be somewhat irritating to some babies and thus interfere with eye contact during bonding, many birth attendants are willing to delay application of the drops until after the parents have had a chance to hold the baby for a while.

In the nursery, babies usually receive a shot of Vitamin K to aid the blood in clotting. Somewhere between the second and fourth days, a drop or two of blood will be drawn from a baby's heel and tested for PKU disease, a rare form of mental retardation which can be prevented if detected and treated early. Many pediatricians routinely order the baby's blood tested for bilirubin level (see page 60). If you have any questions about what is being done for your baby, you should feel free to ask.

CARE OF THE MOTHER AFTER DELIVERY

In the hospital, especially for the first three or four hours after delivery, every mother is watched very carefully. After your baby is born, your blood pressure will be taken several times, and your fundus (uterus) will be checked frequently to make sure that it remains firms. Vaginal flow (lochia) will be checked to make sure it is not excessive. Keep in mind that these procedures are for your protection, even though you may wish you could be left alone to rest without being interrupted. If you are hungry after delivery, don't be afraid to ask for something even if it's not mealtime.

Some women enjoy the opportunity to rest in the hospital. Others find hospital routines to be very irritating. However you feel, try to make the best of your stay, and remember that you'll be leaving soon.

PREMATURE BABIES

Although a baby's internal organs and basic body structure are formed by about the 15th week of pregnancy, many additional weeks inside the mother's uterus are needed for the baby to grow and mature. A full-term pregnancy lasts about 40 weeks from conception to delivery, but about 7% of all newborns arrive early enough to be considered premature.

Although all babies seem to have large heads, a premature baby's head appears to be especially large for the rest of the body. Because sufficient body fat has not yet developed, the baby may appear to be disproportionately long, with spindly limbs. Because a premature baby can't yet regulate body heat, he or she is especially sensitive to temperature changes and must be kept warm. Breathing may be a problem, and some premature babies require supplemental oxygen. If a baby is too small and weak to suck on a nipple, tube feeding must provide the needed nourishment.

The type of care a premature baby needs depends on birth weight and degree of immaturity. If your baby is premature enough to require special care, your doctors will advise you about what is required. Don't be afraid to ask any questions you might have. All babies need loving, caring attention. Even the tiniest premature infant can benefit from being talked to and touched. Ask what you can do to participate in your baby's care. You don't need to (and shouldn't) wait until your baby is big enough to come home to start being a parent.

CIRCUMCISION: YES OR NO?

Circumcision is the surgical removal of the foreskin that normally covers the tip of the penis. If your baby is a boy, one of the first decisions you will have to make is whether or not to have him circumcised. It's best to consider the issues carefully before your baby is born so that your decision will be an informed one.

Because circumcision has been such a widespread practice, many parents assume that it must be done. This is not so. According to the American Academy of Pediatrics, circumcision is a "nonessential surgical procedure" and "... a program of education leading to continuing good personal hygiene would offer all the advantages of routine circumcision without the attendant surgical risk. ..."

There are a number of myths about circumcision that are not supported by facts. Circumcision neither prevents nor causes cancer—either in a man or a woman with whom he has intercourse. There is no proven relationship between circumcision (or lack of it) and sexual pleasure. Circumcision will not prevent or discourage a boy from masturbating.

REASONS FOR CIRCUMCISION

- A circumcised penis may be easier to keep clean.

- If other men in the family are circumcised, the boy will look more like them.

- Among certain religious groups (Jews and Moslems) circumcision is a required ritual.

- If circumcision is later indicated for medical reasons (severe infection, for example) there is a greater risk of psychological trauma from the procedure.

REASONS AGAINST CIRCUMCISION

• It is unnecessary surgery. There are risks involved in the procedure. Hemorrhage may occur. Infection may occur. Although it is very unlikely, the penis can be damaged.

• A program of good hygiene can prevent the same problems that circumcision prevents.

• There is some suffering on the part of the baby, although we don't know for sure how much. Newborns do feel pain, and circumcision is painful.

If you decide against having your baby circumcised, routine bathing and cleansing of the diaper area at changes will be sufficient to keep your little boy clean. Your pediatrician will instruct you if any additional special care is required.

If you decide that you do want your baby circumcised, when to have it done is the next question. A Jewish ritual circumcision is usually done on the eighth day. Most nonritual circumcisions are done before you take the baby home. Some doctors routinely perform circumcisions in the delivery room. While this may be convenient, it is not what's best for your baby. It doesn't make sense to follow the procedures for gentle birth, promote a positive bonding experience, and then immediately inflict the surgical procedure of circumcision on the child. Ask the doctor to wait at least 24 hours before circumcising your newborn. Suggestions for care of the circumcision are on page 50.

NAMING YOUR BABY

As you choose a name for your baby, think over the possibilities very carefully. Don't leave it until the last minute. A hasty decision may not be fair to your child, who will have the name a long time. Be sure to pick a name for a girl and one for a boy (unless, of course, you've had amniocentesis and know for sure which sex your child will be).

FIRST AND MIDDLE NAMES

Here are some guidelines to help you pick the right name for your baby.

• Pick something you really like. Family and cultural traditions often play an important part in choosing a name. Consider names that are especially meaningful in your family or your cultural heritage.

• If you have a fairly common last name, you might be wise to choose a given name that's somewhat more unusual.

• It's safer to avoid names that may be trendy now but potentially silly later. Think about the name carefully. Will it wear well years from now?

• Check out the initials. Make sure they don't spell a vulgar word or one your child might get teased about.

• If etymology (history of words) interests you, there are books available which list names along with their meanings and origins.

LAST NAMES

While most parents choose to have their child use the father's last name, some do not. The child of unmarried parents often uses the mother's name, but this need not be so. In most states it is permissible to choose any surname you wish for your child. Some parents select the mother's maiden name. Others use both parents' names in combination, with a hyphen between them. It is even possible to select a name that is not based on the name of either parent, as long as no fraud is intended.

If you decide to give your child a last name that does not follow the common practice of using the father's surname, it's best to check with the agency that records births in your area (county or municipal clerk, or health department) to find out what special regulations, if any, your state has. If you are planning to do something unusual with your child's name, you might want to tell the doctor ahead of time, so there is no misunderstanding when the official records are being prepared.

BIRTH CERTIFICATE

Shortly after your baby is born, a hospital staff member will probably contact you for information for the baby's birth certificate. If you are ready to name your baby, go ahead and do it. Don't let yourself be pressured into naming your baby, however, if you are not sure of the name you want. Depending on the state in which you live, you have from ten days to seven years to record the child's name on the birth certificate, but once it's recorded, it usually takes a court order to make a change. The space for the name can be left blank until you decide.

Don't be intimidated by a person who is eager to finish the paperwork and close your baby's file. Take the time you need, and choose the name you wish even if it doesn't follow common practice.

THE FIRST FEW DAYS AT HOME

When you first bring your baby home, he or she will sleep, eat, need to be changed, and that's about all. You probably won't feel like doing much more than that either. Fatigue is perhaps one of the most common complaints of a new mother, and it's important for you to rest as much as you can.

WHAT TO DO

Most important, of course, is to tend to your baby's needs. At first, particularly if you are breast-feeding, you may feel as if you're spending most of your time feeding your baby, with a little bit of rest in between feedings. Don't panic. This will change as your baby gains weight and your milk supply becomes established.

The A to Z reference section of this book (pages 35–76) contains information on many topics you may have questions about. The topics in these pages are arranged alphabetically, so you can quickly find what you need. In caring for your baby, do what makes sense to you. There may be several ways to do something. You'll quickly find what works for you and your baby. If you are really concerned about an aspect of your baby's health or well being, and you feel you need further advice, you should call your pediatrician. He or she can reassure you and make certain you're doing the right thing for your baby.

OTHER PEOPLE

How much you involve people other than your immediate family in your first few days at home should be a personal decision. Some mothers do best with household help at this time. Others find the presence of someone else to be an intrusion. If you can afford to hire someone, and you think you would like to do that, we strongly suggest that *you* take care of your baby and let your employee do the cooking, cleaning, and laundry. If your help isn't really helpful, don't be afraid to make a change.

In some families, grandparents can be a wonderful support during the first few days. In others, the parents would prefer to get to know their own child and establish their own routines without other input.

Visitors can be a source of anxiety as well as fatigue during the first few days. It's important that you be able to learn about your new baby without an audience of friends and acquaintances. It's fine to tell people that you need time alone with your baby and to rest. Use doctor's orders as an excuse if you need to.

"THE BLUES"

Postpartum depression, or "the blues," may trouble you during the first week or two. Feelings of depression often accompany the body's attempt to regain its fluid-salt balance after giving birth. If these feelings persist beyond the first two weeks, or you feel overwhelmed by them, call your doctor.

CHOOSING A DOCTOR

Choose your baby's doctor (pediatrician) very carefully. During the years your child is growing up, you will be likely to have many dealings with this person. It's important for you to have confidence in the doctor's professional competence. It's equally important that you feel able to communicate comfortably with him or her. You should share similar philosophies of child rearing.

If this is your first baby, or if your family would like to change pediatricians at this time, you should try to select a doctor well before your new baby arrives. If you have other children, and you are happy about the pediatrician you are currently using, simply tell the doctor's office that you are expecting another baby. Ask how the office should be notified when the baby arrives.

FINDING PEDIATRICIANS

Ask your obstetrician for names of pediatricians who would suit your personal style as well as your baby's needs. Friends or neighbors with young children can tell you about local doctors, although you need not believe everything you hear or agree with their opinions. Call the nearest hospital and ask for names of attending pediatricians. If you plan to breast-feed, La Leche League could tell you which pediatricians are especially supportive to nursing mothers. If cost is a factor, find out about the availability of Well Baby Clinics in your area.

When you've gotten the names of some possible choices, see what you can find out about their training and other qualifications, and their hospital affiliations. Where is the doctor's office located? How would you get there? (Closer is only better if you have transportation.) Call one or two doctors for a consultation appointment. Check out the fees. Are they comparable to others in your area?

MEETING THE DOCTOR

When you meet with the doctor, here are some topics you might wish to bring up. If you have strong personal views on any of these issues, it's best to pick a doctor with whom you agree, or at least one who's neutral and flexible.

• If you plan to use the Leboyer method of gentle birth, does the pediatrician object to, tolerate, or actively support this?

• Does the pediatrician encourage rooming-in for your hospital stay? This may give you some insight into his or her philosophy of newborn care.

• If you and your obstetrician plan an early discharge from the hospital for you, will your pediatrician agree to release the baby (assuming, of course, that all is going well)?

• If your baby is a boy, does the pediatrician recommend circumcision? Why, or why not? If this view is different from your own, will he or she go along with your decision and not pressure you to change it?

• What are the doctor's views on bottle- vs. breast-feeding? Will he or she support you in whatever choice you make?

• When does the doctor generally recommend the introduction of solid foods in a baby's diet? A pediatrician who advocates a very early introduction to solids is unlikely to be fully committed to breast-feeding. A doctor who suggests starting solids for all babies who have reached a certain age, is probably more rigid in approach on other matters than one who makes that decision for each child according to special needs.

• What is the doctor's view on the use of pacifiers (soothers)? If this opinion differs from your own, will he or she support you in your approach?

• If there are any special things about you and your family that a pediatrician should know, this is the time to bring them up. Is your family medical history of interest? Allergies? Blood type? Any history of genetic disorders?

• Are there any cultural or religious practices and beliefs in your family that relate to health care? Are there any medical procedures you would choose to refuse for your child? Do you have any special dietary practices? If you feel strongly about any controversial health care issues, it's best to find a pediatrician with whom you can discuss these things comfortably.

• Is the doctor able and willing to provide guidance in the way that's best for your style of parenting? (Some people want a directive, authoritarian approach that spells out details and orders that things be done in a certain way. Other parents prefer general guidelines within which they can work out routines to suit themselves.) Be sure you choose a doctor whose style meets your needs.

Do you really have to go through all this to find the right pediatrician for your new baby? Maybe, or maybe not. We've provided these guidelines for you to use if you need them. If you are able to work out a good relationship with a pediatrician for your baby with less effort, consider yourself lucky.

FEEDING YOUR BABY

Feeding Your New Baby / Breast Is Best Because... /
Potential Disappointments / The Case for Bottles /
Combining Breast and Bottle / What's Best for You?

Breast-feeding Guide
Prepare During Pregnancy / A Nursing Mother's Diet /
Getting Started (Positions to Try, What to Do, How Long Should
Your Baby Nurse?) / Expressing Your Own Milk (Manual
Expression, Breast Pump) / Storing Your Own Milk / Troubles
and Remedies (Soreness, Engorgement, Poor Let-Down
Reflex, Poor Milk Supply, Hospital Routines, Sleepy or
Disinterested Baby, Frantic Baby) / Special Situations
(Premature Infant, Caesarean Delivery, Twins,
Emergencies) / La Leche League / For More Information

Guide to Bottle Feeding
Kinds of Formula / Needed Equipment / Bottle Preparation
(Modified Method, Terminal Method, Aseptic Method) / Bottle-
Feeding Hints (Preparation, Storage, Some Expensive
Shortcuts) / How to Feed / Formula Temperature / Formula
Intolerance / Vitamin and Mineral Supplements (Vitamins,
Iron, Fluoride)

FEEDING YOUR NEW BABY

How you are going to feed your new baby—breast or bottle or both—is an important decision that *you* must make. What you decide to do—and why—really shouldn't concern anyone but you, your baby, and your baby's father. Nevertheless, chances are good that it will. Most expectant mothers find themselves an easy target for questions and advice from friends, relatives, casual acquaintances, and even strangers. You'll probably do well to ignore the unsolicited comments from others, no matter how well-intentioned they may be. Read the next few pages to help you sort out facts from nonfacts. Then make the decision that's best for you and your family.

BREAST IS BEST BECAUSE...

There are many reasons to choose breast-feeding as the way to nourish a baby. Here are some of them.

• A human mother's milk is the perfect natural food for a human baby. It contains the nutrients baby needs, in the right proportions.

• Breast milk is clean and healthy. Unlike formula, it can't be prepared incorrectly, spoiled in storage, or served in unclean containers.

• Colostrum (the pre-milk breast fluid designed to be baby's first food) contains antibodies to protect against a wide variety of diseases. Colostrum helps clear the meconium (first bowel movement) from the baby's intestines soon after birth.

• Substances in mothers' milk seem to protect babies from certain respiratory and intestinal infections. Breast-fed babies are less likely to suffer from diarrhea or vomiting.

• There are no known allergies to breast milk, although as many as one in ten babies may show some signs of allergic reaction to certain cow's milk formulas.

• Breast milk is easier for a baby to digest fully.

• The exercise of sucking at the breast promotes healthy tooth and jaw development.

• Breast-fed babies tend to swallow less air than bottle-fed babies. They may need to be burped less often and they are less likely to have discomfort from bubbles. The soiled diapers of a breast-fed baby don't have as strong an odor as the diapers of a bottle-fed baby.

• Some mothers feel that night feedings are easier. The baby can be fed and everyone can go back to sleep with a minimum of disruption. However, this is a matter of personal opinion, and it may or may not be true in your case.

• Other than the cost of a nutritious diet for the mother, breast milk is free. Commercial formulas are expensive. You don't have to go shopping for breast milk. It requires no storage and no special equipment for preparation or serving. It's always ready.

• For most mothers, breast-feeding—*after* it has been well established—is easier and more convenient. Wherever mother is, her baby's dinner is too.

• Breast-feeding can be an extremely sensuous and pleasurable experience for a mother as well as for her baby.

• Nursing can have positive emotional benefits for both mother and baby. The continuous contact between a breast-fed baby and the mother provides ideal conditions for strong bonding.

POTENTIAL DISAPPOINTMENTS

It all seems so easy. Your baby is delivered. You put the baby to the breast. The baby knows just what to do. You know just what to do. It's easy and perfectly natural. You and the baby enjoy bonding, you work out a little routine for feedings, and live happily ever after. Right? Well, maybe, and maybe not.

In today's world, there are many pressures which may make breast-feeding less easy for some mothers. It's still perfectly natural, but it may be a bit difficult. A new mother more than 100 years ago wouldn't have had such problems. She would have seen many other women nursing their babies. She would have had role models to follow and lots of experienced help available. She wouldn't have had anyone trying to discourage her from feeding her baby at the breast, for there wasn't any other way. She breast-fed or her baby starved.

Now, however, there are easy alternatives to breast-feeding that would be fine for most mothers and babies. Because of this, there is not as universal or strong a support system for a nursing mother as there was when it was truly a matter of life and death. So if you choose breast-feeding now as the way to nourish your new baby, you may have to work harder at it in the beginning. Most mothers who do find it well worth the effort.

THE CASE FOR BOTTLES...

While mothers' milk will always be the perfect food for babies, the commercial formula available today—if used correctly—provides excellent nourishment. The problems associated with use of formula in underdeveloped countries (contaminated water, unclean equipment, improper formula preparation) are not an issue in situations where people are better informed and sanitary conditions prevail. Here are reasons some women prefer to bottle-feed right from the start.

• Anyone can give the baby a bottle. The continuous presence of the mother at every feeding is not required. The baby's father can be actively involved in feeding the baby.

• It takes somewhat longer for a baby to digest cow's milk. So a bottle-fed baby may sleep a bit longer between feedings than a baby who's breast-fed.

• With a bottle, you can be sure of the quantity your baby is getting.

• Some currently available commercial formulas, although costly, are very convenient. Prepacked single-use bottles require no measuring, no mixing, no special storage, and no heating.

• Although many nursing mothers find that middle-of-the-night feedings are easier because they don't have to go fetch a bottle, other mothers feel that the opportunity to turn nighttime feedings over to the baby's father is a plus for using bottles.

• While a woman would feel comfortable giving her baby a bottle anywhere, some mothers prefer not to breast-feed anywhere but at home. These feelings can cut down on mobility in the early weeks when baby needs very frequent feedings.

• Bottle-feeding requires less support from your family or pediatrician and less effort on your part in the beginning to make it work. (This would not be true, of course, if your baby is one of those with an allergic reaction to formula.)

COMBINING BREAST AND BOTTLE

Is it possible to combine breast-feeding your baby with bottle-feeding and be successful at it? A breast-feeding purist would answer a firm "No!" and counsel against ever letting an artificial nipple anywhere near your baby's mouth. However, by choice or through necessity, many mothers have worked out a system that combines both, and you may decide to do that too. Can you succeed? If your baby is well nourished, and if you and your baby are content with what you're doing, then you're successful. You needn't rate your accomplishment using other people's guidelines.

There's very little available for you to read about combining breast- and bottle-feeding. Most of the books on breast-feeding are enthusiastically and emphatically committed to it as a total approach. Some of the books may even leave you feeling a bit guilty if you consider trying to feed your baby any other way. This is not as it should be. Your life may not fit perfectly into other people's suggestions. Do what works best for you and your baby.

• If you want to breast-feed, give it a wholehearted try. Follow the suggestions on pages 18–28. Skip the pages on using formula.

• *After* your milk supply is well established, no harm will come from giving a bottle for an occasional feeding or even a regularly scheduled feeding each day. The best source of milk, of course, is you. See the directions for expressing and storing your own milk (pages 21–22).

If you use supplementary bottles *before* your milk supply is well established, chances are it never will be. By 6 to 8 weeks you may find that your baby is taking far more milk from the bottle than from your breasts. However, some women find this to be a perfectly satisfactory arrangement.

Gradually phasing out breast-feeding can be far more comfortable for a mother than having to "dry up" in the hospital. And a baby who gets some breast milk—even for a few weeks—does receive some of the benefits only mother's milk can supply. If you do breast-feed your baby for a while and supplement with bottles, don't feel that you have "failed" as a nursing mother. If your baby is thriving, you are both doing fine.

WHAT'S BEST FOR YOU?

Breast milk has many benefits for babies. However, today's commercial formulas do provide satisfactory nutrition for most babies. Most babies can thrive on either. How should you choose?

If you have any interest in breast-feeding at all, we suggest that you prepare for it and try it. Even if you only breast-feed for a few weeks, your baby will get some of the special benefits that are available only in mother's milk. You can always change your mind and switch to bottles if you decide that breast-feeding is not the best way for you and your baby. On the other hand, if you begin with bottles and change your mind, you *could* try to establish breast-feeding later, but it would be very, very difficult.

There are some women for whom breast-feeding is not a wise choice. If the idea of it makes you very uncomfortable or repulses you in any way, you probably shouldn't try it. Even if you're willing to make an effort for your baby's sake, your strong negative feelings would be likely to communicate to the baby. You'd probably do better to begin with bottles and make sure that you give your baby lots of holding and cuddling along the way.

If you want to breast-feed but your husband is very opposed to the idea, encourage him to read pages 14–28. If he is still strongly against the idea of you breast-feeding the baby, and you feel that this will be a continuing source of conflict, you'd probably do better to begin with bottle-feeding. If he wants you to bottle-feed so he can share the feeding chores with you, remember that there's far more to nurturing a baby than getting the milk in. The baby's father can take an active role in holding the baby before and after feedings, changing and burping the baby, and rocking him or her back to sleep. With a breast-fed baby, both parents can still be very close to the baby and involved in his or her care.

If you have to return to work very soon after the birth of your baby, you may choose to bottle-feed right from the start. Some working mothers, however, do nurse their babies for a month or two before switching to bottles. There are benefits for a baby in even a few weeks of breast-feeding. With enough support and encouragement, some mothers do manage to combine working with breast-feeding. This takes a lot of effort, but it can be done. If you seriously wish to combine breast-feeding your new baby with an early return to your job, perhaps the best source of information and guidance would be your local La Leche League. (See page 27.)

Whatever you decide to do, give it your best effort. Remember that being a good mother involves far more than the means by which you get food to your new baby. It's the entire relationship between you and your baby—how you help your baby to love, and learn, and feel secure—that matters. You can be a good mother regardless of whether you use breast, bottle, or a combination of the two methods.

BREAST-FEEDING GUIDE

PREPARE DURING PREGNANCY

If you plan to breast-feed, or even if you think there's a chance you might decide to, you should begin to prepare your breasts for nursing about two months before your baby is due. Women who prepare their breasts tend to be more successful at nursing than those who don't. Preparation is especially important if your skin is fair and sensitive. Here are some tips for getting ready.

(1) Wear a good nursing bra beginning at the seventh month or so. It should fit and support you well. Leave the flaps down for a half hour or more each day. The friction of your outer clothing will help toughen the nipples.

(2) A few minutes of exposure to fresh air and sunlight each day may help. But be careful not to overdo the sun. Sunburn hurts!

(3) Rub your nipples with a terrycloth towel at least twice a day.

(4) Wash your nipples with water, but avoid soap if your nipples tend to be dry. Use cream or oil on them if you wish. Lanolin is a good conditioner for most women. If you happen to be allergic to wool, avoid lanolin, which is made from it. If your skin tends to be very oily rather than dry, you won't need oil or cream conditioners.

(5) Hold each nipple between your fingers and gently pull and roll it for a minute. Do this at least twice daily.

(6) Daily breast massage is useful. This procedure is the first step in hand-expressing milk, which you may need to do after your baby is born. While you are pregnant, breast massage will help condition the milk ducts and establish the flow of colostrum. Place one hand on each side of a breast, close to the chest wall where the breast is fullest in diameter. Your thumbs should be touching at the top of the breast, and your other fingertips at the bottom. Then slide your hands toward the nipples. Keep firm but gentle pressure. Do this several times.

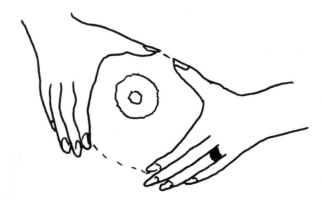

If you are nearing delivery, and you haven't started to prepare your breasts, you can still breast-feed successfully. Many women do very well without any preparation at all. Some women have soreness for a little while no matter how well prepared they are. Careful preparation tips the odds in your favor. It does not guarantee discomfort-free nursing, nor is the failure to prepare a reason to avoid breast-feeding. If you want to breast-feed, you certainly should give it a try, even if you haven't bothered to be diligent about your preparation.

A NURSING MOTHER'S DIET

The balanced diet recommended during pregnancy will serve you well as you breast-feed your new baby. You will need about 1,000 calories of nutritious foods and fluids daily more than what you would require if you were not pregnant or nursing a baby.

Remember that any medications you take can be excreted in your milk. Because of this, a nursing mother should not take any drugs—even over-the-counter items—without consulting the doctor. If you must take a medication, you can minimize its effect on your milk by taking it right after you finish feeding your baby. By the time you begin the next feeding, the level of the drug will be lower.

Sometimes a baby will be sensitive to a particular food the mother eats. There's no point, however, in eliminating from your diet favorite foods that *might* cause a problem until you know that they *do* cause a problem. If you suspect a relationship between a food that you eat and discomfort or fussiness in your baby, then try avoiding that food. Be sensitive to *your* baby's reaction to what you eat, and don't worry in advance about what bothers your friends' children or what you might find on a list of possible problem foods. Let your own baby's responses be your guide, and eat any nutritious food that you want until your baby indicates that you shouldn't.

GETTING STARTED

The best time to begin breast-feeding is as soon as possible after your baby is born, if there haven't been any complications during delivery. (See page 4 for further discussion of this point.) If you are unable to try nursing your baby in the delivery room (because of your condition or because of hospital policy), begin as soon as you are able. Both you and your baby will benefit.

It's natural for a baby to search for the mother's nipple. The "rooting reflex"—something every baby mammal has—helps the baby get what he or she is seeking. Here's how it works. Whenever something touches a newborn's cheek, the baby will turn toward that object and try to put it in the mouth. So if you gently stroke the side of your baby's face nearest you with your nipple, the baby will turn to take hold of the nipple. Don't try to push the little face toward the nipple, because the rooting reflex would then cause your baby to turn toward the pushing hand. You would accomplish the exact opposite of what you set out to do.

Here are some suggestions for putting your baby to the breast at first.

• Relax and have courage. Nursing a newborn is the most natural thing a mother can do. Long before there were "how to" books, mothers were successfully feeding their babies.

• Get comfortable. Try different positions. There is no one right way. Do what seems best for you.

POSITIONS TO TRY

• You can nurse lying down (on the delivery table or in bed). Turn on your side, and raise the arm you are lying on over your head if your wish. Pillows under and behind your head and shoulders will help support you. Some women are most comfortable with a pillow behind the back as well. Put your baby on his or her side facing you, with feet touching your body and mouth near your nipple.

• You can sit in bed with pillows to support your back and arms. Hold your baby cradled in your arms, supporting the neck, head, and shoulders in your bent elbow. Or, if you bend your knees, you might find it comfortable to place your baby on a pillow in your lap.

• Some women, particularly those with large breasts, find the "football position" most comfortable. Hold your baby under your arm the way a running back carries a football. For the left breast, hold your baby in your left arm. Support the head and neck with your left hand. Use your right arm and hand for the right breast.

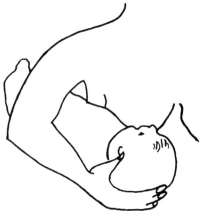

WHAT TO DO

(1) Using your free hand to hold your breast, gently stroke the baby's cheek with the nipple. The rooting reflex will cause your baby to turn with open mouth toward the touch. Guide the nipple into the baby's mouth.

(2) As much of the areola (dark area around the nipple) as possible should be in the baby's mouth. If the baby only gets the tip of the nipple, you'll get sore and the baby won't get much milk. As you put the nipple into the baby's mouth, make sure it is touching the roof of the mouth. This stimulates the baby's sucking reflex and keeps him or her at it.

(3) If the baby isn't getting enough of the areola, remove him or her and start over again. Don't pull or tug to remove a sucking baby from the breast. That hurts. Instead, put your little finger into the corner of the baby's mouth. This breaks the suction so you can move the baby easily.

(4) Be sure that your baby can breathe easily while nursing. If your breasts are big or very full, use a finger to press the breast away from the baby's nostrils while he or she sucks.

(5) Use both breasts at each feeding. At the next feeding, begin with the breast you used last the time before. (To help you remember, tie a ribbon or put a safety pin on the bra strap on the side you finished with.)

HOW LONG SHOULD YOUR BABY NURSE?

How long should your baby nurse at first? To minimize soreness, you'll probably want to limit sucking time at first. However, if you begin with less than five minutes per breast, that won't be very effective either. Very short nursing periods may not be enough to get your breasts to "let down" the milk supply. If this happens, your baby won't get much, your breasts won't know to produce more, and what's left in the breasts may cause you discomfort. One- to two-minute feeds on each breast may prevent first-day soreness, but in most cases it just delays the problem. Unlimited sucking, on the other hand, may be more than most mothers can handle at first. Here's a suggested timetable that works for many mothers.

1st day	5 minutes each side per feeding
2nd day	7–8 minutes each side per feeding
3rd day	10 minutes each side per feeding
4th day	10–12 minutes each side per feeding
5th day and after	15–20 minutes each side per feeding

EXPRESSING YOUR OWN MILK

Expressing your own milk is a useful technique to learn. You may want to express some milk to ease engorgement, or to help your baby get started at the beginning of a feeding. If your baby is in an intensive care nursery, you may be able to express your own milk to provide a supply for your baby's feedings. This will maintain your milk supply so you can breast-feed later. It may be convenient to express and store your own milk so that someone else can give a feeding to your breast-fed baby.

MANUAL EXPRESSION

• Be sure your hands are clean.

• Use a clean container to collect the milk, and lean over the container so that the milk you express will drop into it.

• Hold the outer edge of the areola between your thumb and fingers, as in the picture.

• Squeeze the thumb and fingers together, pulling back toward your chest wall.

At first it may take some practice before you express milk successfully. When your milk supply is well established, you'll probably be able to express several ounces at a time.

BREAST PUMP

If you wish to express and store your milk on a regular basis, you might find using a breast pump to be more satisfactory than manual expression. Some women are able to use successfully a small hand-held pump that directs the milk right into a nursing bottle. These relatively inexpensive devices can be purchased at many pharmacies and baby supply stores. Electric pumps, which are quite costly, can often be rented or borrowed. Ask your physician or contact your local La Leche League for further information.

STORING YOUR OWN MILK

If you plan to feed the milk you've expressed to your baby within 48 hours, simply refrigerate it in its clean container. (Containers washed in a dishwasher will do. If you don't have a dishwasher, wash the container and boil it for five minutes.)

Milk kept longer than 48 hours should be frozen. It will keep about two weeks in the freezer compartment of your refrigerator, and several months in a deep freeze. Freezer containers (at least dishwasher clean) or tightly-tied plastic food bags are satisfactory storage containers for milk. Thaw gradually the milk you plan to use on a given day. Move the frozen milk to the refrigerator for a few hours. You can warm the bottle under the faucet, but don't have the water too hot or the milk might curdle. Shake the bottle before feeding the baby, so the cream mixes back in.

TROUBLES AND REMEDIES

Here are some troubles common to the early days of breast-feeding. You may experience some of them. Hopefully, many of them will pass you by. If not, try the suggestions. Above all, try not to get discouraged. These problems generally don't last.

SORENESS

• Go back and read the suggestions for preparing your nipples (page 18). These techniques are helpful after you begin nursing as well.

• Put the baby to the least sore breast first. By the time you put the baby to the more tender breast, your milk will have let down, and this will help.

• Ask your doctor for advice. Or contact a La Leche League leader. Many women have sore nipples at first. Encouragement will help you to keep trying to nurse until the soreness stops. Be reassured that the problem won't last.

• An oxytocin spray may speed up your let-down reflex. Ask your doctor if this is advisable in your case.

• Above all, avoid the temptation to skip a feeding or cut the time way down (below 4 or 5 minutes). You may hurt less at the time, but you could end up adding engorgement or clogged milk ducts to simple soreness.

ENGORGEMENT

When the milk first comes in, many women have engorged (overfull) breasts. Engorged breasts feel hot, hard, and painful.

• Nurse often. This is the best way to bring relief. It's also the best for your baby.

• Warm water (shower, bath, or hot water bottle) helps some women. Others prefer the opposite approach and use an ice pack.

• Hand-express a little milk before you nurse your baby (see page 21).

• An oxytocin spray might help speed up the let-down reflex. Ask your doctor about this.

• If you feel like you must take a pain reliever, ask your doctor to advise you. Anything you take can affect the baby through your milk, but your doctor may suggest a non-aspirin pain reliever if you really need one.

• Be patient. Engorgement is common right at the beginning. It is seldom a problem as nursing gets well established.

Women who decide *not* to breastfeed often suffer from engorgement for a few days. Hot or cold packs or a mild pain reliever may help. If you don't want to breast-feed and your breasts are engorged, temporarily cut down on fluid intake. Resist the impulse to express milk, because this will only prolong the problem by creating a new supply to meet what your body perceives as a demand.

POOR LET-DOWN REFLEX

No matter how much milk your body can make, it won't do your baby any good unless your let-down reflex works well and the milk flows so your baby can get it. This depends on your mental attitude as well as your physical condition.

You'll probably be able to tell if the let-down reflex is functioning well. At first, let-down will happen about three minutes or so after the baby begins to suck. As breast-feeding becomes well established, some mothers let down when they hear their babies cry for milk. Most mothers feel a tingling sensation and fullness in the breasts, mild contractions of the uterus, and some temporary nipple tenderness when they let down. Milk may leak or even spray forcefully from one or both breasts.

If your let-down reflex isn't working well, your baby won't be getting enough milk. He or she may begin by sucking fiercely, but then will give up when the milk isn't coming. Try these suggestions to help your let-down reflex.

• Have courage. Try to relax. Believe that you're going to do just fine. (If you don't, you probably won't.)

• A glass of wine, beer, or a cocktail about 15 minutes before feeding may help you relax. Check this out with your doctor first. Some women even find a cup of tea relaxing.

• Heat on the breasts may help. Nurse right after a warm bath or shower. Or try a heating pad or hot water bottle.

• Massage each breast before you nurse. (See the directions on page 18.)

• An oxytocin spray might help. Ask your doctor if this is recommended in your case.

POOR MILK SUPPLY

A mother's milk production works on a supply and demand basis. The more the baby sucks (demands), the more milk the mother's body will produce (supply). Signs of a poor milk supply include a fussy baby who seems hungry and produces fewer than six wet diapers a day. (What doesn't go in can't come out.)

If poor milk supply seems to be a problem for you, try these suggestions.

(1) Nurse more often. The more you nurse and your baby sucks, the more milk your body will produce.

(2) Increase your intake of fluids and nutritious foods. Take a glass of fruit juice or something else to drink just before you nurse. Do it every time. This will help insure that you are taking enough. See that your diet contains enough protein and calcium.

(3) Try the suggestions under Let-Down Reflex (page 23).

HOSPITAL ROUTINES

Many women find that they are too uncomfortable with hospital routines to begin to breast-feed successfully while still in the hospital. Many mothers do not get going with a good feeding routine until they take their babies home. If being in the hospital is making it difficult for you to manage breast-feeding your new baby, here are some suggestions.

(1) If you are doing well, and you have help at home, early discharge might be the answer. This is something to discuss with your obstetrician and the baby's pediatrician.

(2) Make sure that all members of the nursery staff know that your baby is being breast-fed. If you do not wish your baby to receive any artificial nipples, ask your pediatrician to note this on your baby's chart.

(3) Rooming-in, if you can afford it and if the facilities are available, is the best choice for successful in-hospital start of breast-feeding.

(4) Be willing to feed your baby every two hours if necessary. If the nursery staff prefers a 3- to 4-hour schedule, go fetch your baby more often if it's possible to do so.

(5) Make it clear that you wish to be awakened for your baby's nighttime feedings. This is another thing that should be noted by the doctor on your baby's chart.

(6) See if you can find a nursery staff nurse who is especially supportive if you need help. One who has herself been a successful nursing mother may be able to give you the help you need.

(7) Even in the hospital, a La Leche League leader can be contacted for assistance.

(8) Try to ignore any negative comments from nurses or other mothers who are opposed to breast-feeding. Your baby is your own. What they think doesn't matter, and it won't unless you let it.

(9) Be cheered by the fact that you're not going to be in the hospital very long. As soon as you and your baby get home, you can do things your way.

SLEEPY OR DISINTERESTED BABY

Sometimes it appears that a baby just isn't interested in working at getting milk from the mother's breast. What should you do if this is the case with your baby?

• First of all, don't feel rejected. You haven't failed. During the first couple of days, many babies are sleepy and not too interested in nursing. This is especially true for babies whose mothers were medicated during labor and delivery, but may be the case in other babies as well.

• If your baby is brought to you in the hospital and he or she doesn't seem interested in nursing, use the time to get to know your baby instead. Hold and cuddle the baby. Let him or her get used to the sound of your voice. Relax.

• While some babies suck beautifully right from the start, others seem to need instruction in getting on with it. Help your baby to find the nipple if necessary. Stroke your baby's cheek nearest you with the nipple. The rooting reflex will make the head turn toward your touch.

• Be sure to tilt your nipple slightly upward as the baby puts it in the mouth. The touch of the nipple on the roof of the baby's mouth stimulates the sucking reflex.

• In the hospital, if your baby is sleepy when brought to you for a feeding, try to wake the baby up before you begin. This is particularly likely to happen if the hospital follows a set feeding schedule and does not bring babies to mothers on demand. See if you can arrange to have your baby brought to you when he or she is hungry, rather than when the clock says it is time. If this is impossible, be reassured that you'll do much better when you get your baby home.

• Make sure your baby isn't getting bottles in the nursery. A baby who isn't hungry isn't likely to bother with trying to get milk from the mother.

• For a baby who isn't eager to suck, don't offer a pacifier in the mistaken notion that it will teach effective sucking behavior. The best way for you to teach your baby to suck well is to offer yourself at frequent intervals.

• Sometimes a baby will nurse for two or three minutes and then fall asleep again. Wake the baby. Change the diaper if needed. A cool, damp cloth on the face or soles of the feet may be effective. Talk to your baby and play with him or her. Then try to nurse again.

• Sometimes a little milk hand-expressed into a reluctant baby's mouth will get things started.

• If you feel that you need more help, it's important to get it before you become discouraged. Call a La Leche League representative if you have questions and want reassurance.

FRANTIC BABY

While some babies seem to be sleepy at what the hospital schedules as feeding time, others may be upset and crying. What should you do if your baby is crying frantically when he or she is brought to you?

• Before you start to nurse, calm the baby down if you can. Hold and rock your baby. Talk to him or her.

• A vigorously crying baby may be swallowing air. Sometimes you'll have to burp the baby before starting to feed.

• If the baby is crying because he or she is very hungry, getting the nursing going is, of course, the best remedy. But sometimes a baby is just too frantic to suck. If you relax, you have a better chance of getting your baby calmed down for the meal.

SPECIAL SITUATIONS

PREMATURE INFANT

If your baby is premature, you may have to wait a while until breast-feeding. Discuss your baby's special needs with your pediatrician. Many doctors, however, feel that breast milk is best for a premature baby. If your newborn is in an intensive care unit, you may be asked to express milk for him or her.

If you want to nurse your premature baby when he or she is able, then you should begin to express milk from your breasts a day or so after delivery. (See page 21.) This will build up your milk supply so that it will be there when your baby is ready. If you're not supplying your own baby with the milk, you may wish to donate it to a milk bank or freeze it for your baby's use later.

For guidance on what's best for you and your baby, talk to your doctor. La Leche League may be of assistance too.

CAESAREAN DELIVERY

If your baby has been delivered by Caesarean section, you can nurse just as successfully as a woman who has delivered vaginally. Your breasts will make milk either way. Discomfort from the incision might make it a little harder for you to find a comfortable position at first. The first day or two, you might need help putting the baby to the breast. You'll probably have to stay in the hospital a bit longer if you have a Caesarean, so you won't be able to settle into a routine at home quite as quickly. You'll need lots of rest. These are minor irritations, however. Don't be discouraged. If you want to breast-feed your baby, a Caesarean delivery in no way means that you shouldn't or can't.

TWINS

It's not only possible to breast-feed twins, it's probably a lot easier (and certainly cheaper) than preparing a double set of bottles each day. The extra stimulation two sucking babies provide will, in most cases, insure an abundant supply of milk.

Most mothers of twins find it's most efficient to nurse both babies at the same time. A complete demand schedule for each individual baby could result in an exhausted mother who has time for nothing other than feeding her babies. So when the more demanding of the two babies wants to eat, it's a good time to feed them both. Try to alternate breasts so that a baby doesn't get hooked on just one side. This is especially important if your babies tend to take significantly different amounts.

You'll have to experiment to find the best position for nursing twins. The football position (one baby under each arm with feet behind you) works well. You might try crisscrossing your babies in your lap, with one over the other. Try out different ways until you find what's most comfortable for all of you.

EMERGENCIES

Sometimes a nursing mother and her baby must be temporarily separated for reasons beyond their control. For example, either mother or baby might have to be hospitalized. Some hospitals will permit a nursing mother to be with her baby for feedings. If not, or if the condition of either makes that impossible, it still may be possible to resume breast-feeding later.

Continue production of your milk supply by expressing milk (see page 21) until you and your baby can be reunited. Sometimes another nursing mother can take over feeding your baby until you can do it again. La Leche League may be able to help you find someone. Or your baby can be bottle-fed during your absence. If so, it may take a bit of effort to get the baby used to the breast again.

If you don't maintain your milk supply while you and your baby are separated, it still may be possible to begin lactation again. This will take considerable hard work and perseverance.

LA LECHE LEAGUE

La Leche League is an organization that provides information and encouragement to any woman who wishes to breast-feed. Volunteers are available throughout the country to help you with problems that arise as you are breast-feeding your new baby. The League's publications include a book, *Womanly Art of Breastfeeding,* and a newsletter, *La Leche League News.*

For further information, including the names, addresses, and phone numbers of your nearest La Leche League representatives, you can write to:

La Leche League International, Inc.
9616 Minneapolis Avenue
Franklin Park, Illinois 60131

Most La Leche League leaders are enthusiastically committed to the belief that every baby should be breast-fed and that every woman can nurse successfully.

It's quite all right to ask La Leche League for support and information even if you don't accept the entire philosophy offered along with it. You can ask for help and advice even if you don't agree with all of it. For example, you don't have to keep all supplemental bottles out of the house, or nurse your baby through toddlerhood unless that's what *you* really want to do. Don't be put off by the occasional overzealousness or personal excess on the subject of breast-feeding you may find with an individual volunteer. If the assistance offered seems a bit too pushy for your personal style, just keep remembering that it's *your* baby. La Leche League performs a valuable service. Accept graciously what's helpful to you, and don't feel guilty about doing things your way.

FOR MORE INFORMATION

In these pages, we've tried to present some of the information a new mother who wishes to breast-feed will find helpful. Some women will find this to be all the written material they want or need. Others will not. In preparation for nursing your new baby you might wish to read one or more of the other books available. Here are some suggestions.

The Complete Book of Breastfeeding
Marvin S. Eiger, M.D. and **Sally Wendkos Olds**
Bantam Books, New York: 1987

A thorough and supportive text with topics ranging from "Should You or Shouldn't You" to "Weaning Your Baby." In addition to the "how to" chapters for the mother, there is one written for the father to enlist his support.

The Experience of Breastfeeding
Sheila Kitzinger
Penguin Books, New York: 1987

An excellent book which deals in considerable depth with the social, emotional, and psychosexual aspects of the mother-baby relationship, as well as with the "how to's" of breast-feeding. This book isn't easy reading, but if the emotional aspects of being a breast-feeding woman are of interest to you, there's material here you won't find in most other books.

Nursing Your Baby
Karen Pryor
Pocket Books, New York: 1984

A comprehensive book on breast-feeding, recommended by La Leche League. This book is strongly committed to the notion that breast-feeding is *the* way to feed a baby. Many women find this book extremely helpful and supportive. A few, however, might find themselves feeling a bit guilty if things don't work out that way for them.

Please Breast-Feed Your Baby
Alice Girard, with an introduction by **C. D. Haagensen, M.D.**
Signet Books, New American Library, New York: 1970

Supportive and pleasant to read text. This book provides information along with plenty of encouragement for a mother in today's world.

Preparation for Breast Feeding
Donna and **Rodger Ewy**
Dolphin Books, Doubleday & Co., New York: 1985

An informative and supportive book. Useful information is provided in the context of breast-feeding as a family-centered experience. The importance of encouragement and support for a successful experience is stressed.

GUIDE TO BOTTLE FEEDING

If you've decided to bottle-feed your new baby, your pediatrician will advise you about what formula to use. If the brand used in the hospital agreed with your baby, you'll probably be told to stay with that one. Many hospitals let a new mother take home a sample pack of prefilled bottles. These will help you get through the first day or so.

KINDS OF FORMULA

For routine feeding of healthy, normal newborns, the major brands of commercially prepared formulas available in the United States are Enfamil, Similac, and SMA. These are similar in characteristics to mother's milk. Use the one your doctor recommends. If your baby is doing well, don't switch brands.

It doesn't matter which size container you buy, as long as you prepare and use the formula as directed. Prefilled bottles and 8 oz., ready-to-serve cans are the most expensive. The large (32 oz.) cans of ready-to-serve formula cost less per ounce than the smaller cans. Large cans of concentrate or powder are the least expensive, but they require preparation.

Concocting your own formula from evaporated milk and additives will take a lot of time and effort. You will not save much money over the cost of commercially prepared mixes. And what you'll end up with will not be as similar to mother's milk as a commercially prepared formula would be. So we don't recommend blending your own formula. If you're going to bottle-feed, use one of the commercially prepared formulas. If expense is a problem for you, be sure to use the most economical forms. Buy large cans of concentrate and stay away from prefilled bottles or small cans of ready-to-use.

> If you want to read more about nourishing your new baby, a good resource is **No-Nonsense Nutrition for your Baby's First Year,** by Jo-Ann Heslin, Annette B. Natow, and Barbara C. Raven (Bantam Books, New York: 1980). The authors are trained nutritionists as well as mothers, and the book contains a wealth of information.

NEEDED EQUIPMENT

You will need about a dozen bottles in all. Here are some things to consider before you buy.

- Plastic is safer than glass. Today's plastic bottles are dishwasher-safe, boilable, and they won't break when you drop them.

- For most newborns, 4 oz. bottles are large enough. You may need to switch to 8 oz. bottles fairly soon, and many mothers prefer to start with the large ones. Others prefer to stick with the smaller bottles, which are lighter and easier to store. You can always offer two small bottles at a feeding when your baby is taking more than four ounces, if you don't want to use large bottles. Do whatever makes the most sense to you.

- Get the nipples, collars, and caps that go with the bottles. Although most brands are interchangeable, some are not. A few extra nipple sets will be very handy when you can't find enough pieces to go around or when you drop one on the floor just before feeding the baby.

- If you use nursers with disposable liners, get at least a week's supply in advance. You'll need 6–8 per day at first.

No matter what kind of bottles you buy, you'll need a bottle brush and a nipple brush to keep them clean. This is true even if you have a dishwasher. You need something that gets into the corners to make sure the milk deposits are out.

Some pediatricians recommend the use of Nuk nipples, which are designed with the shape of the baby's palate in mind. A Nuk nipple is relatively squashy, which makes it easier for a baby to control the rate of milk flow. If you do use Nuk nipples, remember that there's an up side and a down side to each one. You must put it in the baby's mouth correctly. This is a bit of information that anyone who feeds your baby will have to have.

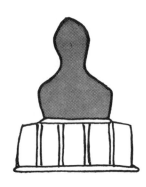

Before you invest in a complete set of any one kind of bottles and nipples, you might want to try different ones to see which work best for you and your baby. It's easy to do this if you use the prefilled bottles for the first couple of days while you're making up your mind.

BOTTLE PREPARATION

Must you sterilize your baby's bottles? Doctors differ on the answer to this question. Some pediatricians still recommend that you sterilize bottles for the first two or three months. Others believe that modern refrigeration, a clean water supply, commercial formula, and care in bottle cleaning and preparation all add up to safety for your baby without having to sterilize. Unless your doctor directs you to use a different method of preparing formula, we suggest that you use a modified method of preparation which makes sure things are clean, although not necessarily sterile.

MODIFIED METHOD

Make sure the bottles (nipples, caps, etc.) are clean and dry. Dishwasher clean is ideal. A hot soapy wash with a bottle brush and a good rinse will do.

- The can opener and the top of the can should be clean too.

- If you use a formula that requires water for preparation, ask the doctor if your tap water is O.K. In many areas it will be. If not, boil it for two minutes.

- Put the formula into the bottles. Add the right amount of water if you're using a concentrated formula base. Don't dilute ready-to-serve formula.

• Put the nipples, collars, and protective caps on the bottles. Store in the refrigerator. Use within 24 hours.

If your pediatrician insists that you sterilize the bottles for your newborn, here are two ways to do it. The terminal method involves putting formula into bottles and then sterilizing the filled bottles. The aseptic method involves putting sterile formula into sterilized equipment.

TERMINAL METHOD

• The bottles should be clean—washed by hand with hot soapy water and rinsed well, or done in the dishwasher.

• Mix the formula according to the directions. You may use cold tap water.

• Fill the bottles. Put a nipple upside down on each bottle and put the collars and caps on loosely so the steam can get to all the parts.

• Put the bottles in a sterilizer or large pot. Add water until it's about one-third the way up the bottles. If the bottles are close together, they won't fall over when the boiling water bounces them around.

• Cover the pot, bring the water to a boil, and let it boil for 20 minutes.

• Leave the cover on, and let the water cool gradually for at least an hour or two. (If you try to speed up the gradual cooling, skin may form on top of the formula and clog the nipples.)

• Take the bottles out. Fasten the caps tightly. Refrigerate and use within 48 hours.

ASEPTIC METHOD

• If you need water to prepare the formula, boil it for at least two minutes.

• Get the equipment ready. Boil everything (bottles, nipples, collars, caps, measuring tools, can opener, tongs, etc.) in a covered pot for 20 minutes.

• Get the formula ready. If you have to mix it, you can do it in one batch in a sterile container, or one bottle at a time.

• Put the formula into the bottles. Put on the nipples, collars, and caps. Refrigerate the bottles and use them within 48 hours.

BOTTLE-FEEDING HINTS

PREPARATION

• Be sure that the tool you use to open the can is clean. (The remains of yesterday's dog food don't belong in your baby's formula.) The safest practice is to have one opener just for your baby's formula and to clean it along with the bottles.

• If the quality of your water supply is questionable, using ready-to-serve formula will eliminate the boiling water step from formula preparation.

• Be very careful to use canned formula correctly. If it is ready-to-serve, do not dilute it with water. (Adding a little water to make it last longer could harm your baby's health.) If you use a concentrated formula base, be sure to add the correct amount of water as directed. (Double strength formula is not twice as good—it can make your baby uncomfortable or sick.)

• Sterile nipples, collars, and caps can be stored in a glass canning jar with a screwtop lid.

STORAGE

• If you have trouble keeping track of how long a bottle has been in the refrigerator, try labeling as you prepare. That way you'll know for sure if that bottle behind the leftovers is from last night or last week. Jot the date on little sticky labels and apply one to each bottle before you store it.

• If you have any doubts about a bottle of formula, discard it. It's cheaper (as well as a lot better for your baby) to throw out some formula than to need a doctor when your baby gets sick from spoiled formula.

• If the baby doesn't finish a bottle within a hour or so of starting it, throw it out. Don't keep partially consumed bottles for future feedings. A little saliva in the bottle, along with lack of refrigeration for a period of time are fine for harmful bacteria, and not fine for your baby.

• If your baby routinely leaves the bottles unfinished, and you are throwing out quite a bit of formula, just prepare each bottle with less to begin with.

SOME EXPENSIVE SHORTCUTS

• The easiest bottles to use are the single-use, prefilled ones. They are absolutely safe, and require no preparation. Simply open and use. Most supermarkets don't carry them, so you may have to try a pharmacy. These bottles are expensive, but a wonderful luxury.

• Most brands of formula are available in ready-to-use, 8 oz. cans. Simply open the can with a clean opener and pour the formula into a clean bottle or two. The small cans are more expensive, but they are especially convenient for preparing one or two bottles at a time, for traveling, and when refrigeration facilities are not handy.

• Some mothers like nursing bottles with disposable bag liners. The lining is discarded after use, and ordinary washing is sufficient for the bottle that holds the liner. Complete directions for use of nursers with liners can be found on the package. Have a regular bottle or two handy in case you run out of liners

• Single-use nipples, each in a sterile package, can be purchased in bulk. These are expensive, but very handy for traveling because they require no special care. Just open, use, and throw away when baby is done.

HOW TO FEED

When you give your baby a bottle, be sure to serve comfort, security, and emotional nourishment along with the milk. Cradle your baby in your arm, with your bent elbow supporting the head and neck. An alternate position that both of you might like is with the baby propped facing you in your lap. Remember that feeding times are the highlights of a newborn baby's day. Holding your baby for feeding is an important part of developing a close relationship. It's important that anyone who takes a turn feeding the baby keep these suggestions in mind.

- The baby shouldn't be lying flat on the back for feeding. The baby's head should be at a level at least slightly higher than his or her tummy.

- Never prop the bottle and leave the baby. A baby can choke or suffocate while feeding this way. In addition to being dangerous, the practice of propping a bottle deprives a baby of the human contact that's important for emotional security and well-being.

- Check the nipple of the bottle before feeding. When you hold the bottle upside down, the milk should drip out in little drops.

- As you are feeding, make sure the baby is getting milk. You'll notice little bubbles moving along inside the bottle if the milk is getting through the nipple.

- Keep the bottle tilted so that the neck of the bottle is always filled with milk. If you don't, your baby will swallow too much air.

- To increase the flow of milk, loosen the nipple collar slightly. If this doesn't do it, larger nipple holes might be needed. (Use a hot needle to enlarge the hole. Hold a lighted match to the point of the needle for a moment.)

- To slow down the flow, tighten the nipple collar. Boiling a nipple for a few minutes may help close up holes that are too large. If this doesn't work, you'll have to start again with new nipples.

- A feeding should take about 20 minutes. If it takes a lot longer, or if the baby is only taking an ounce or two in this time and wants to be fed again soon, make sure the nipple holes are large enough.

- Be sure to burp your baby often enough during a feeding. To be on the safe side at first, try it after every ounce. (See page 45.)

FORMULA TEMPERATURE

Heating a baby's bottle before serving used to be standard procedure. Many people still like to do it. You may heat your baby's bottle if you wish, but it's not necessary or even better to do it. Most hospital nurseries serve the bottles at room temperature.

Studies have been done to find out what temperature formula is best for baby. It doesn't seem to matter whether the formula is warm, room temperature, or right out of the refrigerator. Babies who were studied seemed to thrive equally well no matter which temperature formula was used.

What should you do for your baby? If your baby has a preference, do what your baby likes. If your baby doesn't have a preference, do what makes sense to you. Cool formula in hot weather and warm formula in cold weather might work well. If you do choose to warm your baby's bottle, make sure you don't overdo it. Test the milk on the inside of your wrist before serving, to make sure it won't burn your baby's mouth. You don't need to buy a bottle warmer. A pan of warm water will do it.

If you decide not to bother with bottle warming, be prepared for comments from people who raised their children when warm milk was thought to be a must. You are not being careless or lazy by serving your baby an unwarmed bottle, and anyone who suggests that you are just doesn't know any better. Smile sweetly, and do as you please.

FORMULA INTOLERANCE

If your baby is doing well on the formula you are using, don't switch brands. It's best not to tamper with success. If, however, your baby is continually fussy or irritable, with spitting up or vomiting, it's possible that the formula is causing the difficulty.

Some babies, for example, can't tolerate the formula with iron supplement added, and they require the iron-free version. Some babies are allergic to cow's milk with or without iron, and they must be fed using a milk-free formula. These babies are usually placed on formula made from soy protein.

If you suspect that the formula you are using is causing your baby difficulty, consult the baby's pediatrician. It's best to work with the doctor on solving the problem rather than attempting to change the baby's diet on your own.

VITAMIN AND MINERAL SUPPLEMENTS

VITAMINS

Breast-fed babies of well-nourished mothers usually get an adequate supply of vitamins from their mother's milk. The exception to this is Vitamin D, which may be prescribed. Most infant vitamin products combine vitamins, and it won't harm your baby to get the others in the supplement along with the D, as long as you stick to the recommended dosage.

IRON

Most infants are born with about a three-month supply of stored iron. Although breast milk contains a little iron, what it does contain is easily used by a nursing baby, and in most cases, iron supplements are not necessary. If a supplement is required, the pediatrician will let you know. An iron-fortified formula may be used for a bottle-fed baby who requires an additional supply of iron.

FLUORIDE

If your water supply contains less than 0.3 parts per million of fluoride, the doctor may prescribe a fluoride supplement (available separately and in liquid vitamins) for your baby. Some doctors recommend this supplement within the first few weeks. Others do not start it until the baby is several months old. If your water supply is fluoridated to a level of 1 part per million, do not use a fluoride supplement for your baby. Too much can be toxic and cause harm.

SECTION THREE

THINGS TO KNOW, FROM A TO Z

Accidents (First Aid: Artificial Respiration, Bites, Bleeding, Burns, Choking, Convulsions, Falls) / Accidents (Prevention) / Air Quality / Automobile Safety / Babyproofing / Babysitters / Baths (Sponge Baths, Tub Baths, Shampoos) / Books / Bowel Movements / Breathing / Burping and Bubbles / Car Beds / Car Restraints / Carriages and Strollers / Carrier (Basket, Soft Front Pack) / Changing the Baby / Circumcision Care / Clothing / Colic / Constipation / Cradle Cap / Crib Bumpers / Crib Death / Cribs / Crying / Diapers (Choices, Cloth, Disposable) / Diaper Rash / Diarrhea / Fever / Furniture for Baby / Heat Rash (Prickly Heat) / Jaundice / Laundry / Layette / Lighting / Mobiles / Nail Care / Noise / Outings / Pacifiers (Soothers) / Skin Rashes / Sleeping / Solid Foods / Spitting Up / Sucking Needs / Swaddling / Temperature (of Baby's Room) / Temperature (Taking Baby's) / Thrush / Toys / Travel (Air Travel, Train Travel, Bus Travel) / Twins / Vomiting / Zippers

ACCIDENTS (First Aid)

Although care and common sense will help prevent most accidents (see page 39), there's always the chance that something might go wrong. We hope you never need to use any of the following first aid techniques, but we've included them just in case.

ARTIFICIAL RESPIRATION

Use these steps only if the baby has stopped breathing for more than ten seconds, and don't waste any time getting on with it. (Never give artificial respiration to a person who is breathing.) Continue until the baby is breathing well on his or her own, or until expert help gets there.

If drowning caused the problem, begin with Step 1. If not, begin with Step 2.

(1) First get the water out of the baby's lungs. To do this, hold the baby face down with the head lower than the rest of the body.

(2) Use a hooked finger to clear the baby's mouth of mucus, food, or anything else that shouldn't be there.

(3) Place the baby on his or her back, on a flat surface.

(4) Tilt the baby's head back (neck stretched, chin up, jaw forward) to keep the air passages open.

(5) With your mouth, cover the baby's mouth and nose tightly. Breathe a small puff of air gently into the baby's nose and mouth just enough to make the chest wall move up a little. (Remember that a newborn is very small, and couldn't handle the entire contents of your lungs at once.)

(6) Move away so the air can come out. Put your mouth back to the baby and breathe another puff of air; then move away. Do this every three seconds (20 times a minute) until the baby begins to breathe well or help comes.

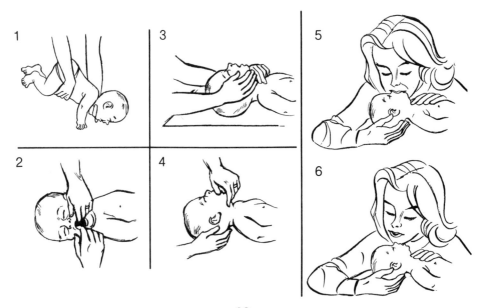

BITES (Animal or Human)

Wash the area well with soap and water. If it is not bleeding badly, let the water run gently over it for a few minutes. When the bleeding has stopped, cleanse with Mercurochrome and cover the wound with a sterile dressing. Call the doctor for advice the same day.

BITES (Insect)

If there's a stinger, it's probably best to leave it alone and let the doctor remove it. Touching it may release more venom and increase the reaction. If you must remove the stinger on your own, scrape it out with a fingernail. You may get a wee bit of skin, but that's preferable to leaving the stinger in there. A little meat tenderizer and water on the bite may help draw out the venom. Check this out with the doctor. Apply cold compresses, and watch the baby carefully for any reaction to the bite. Call the doctor right away if the baby becomes pale or weak, or develops a rash or hives, fever, trouble breathing, nausea, or vomiting.

BLEEDING

Stop bleeding from cuts or bites by direct pressure applied for 5 to 10 minutes continuously. An ice cube in a clean cloth may help. If this doesn't work, get medical attention right away. Continue to apply pressure to the injury until help comes.

BURNS

Cool the injured area as fast as possible by dunking the burned part in cold water or applying cold compresses to the area. Continue to apply cold for several minutes until the pain stops. Then pat the skin dry very gently with the cleanest cloth or towel you can find. Keep the area covered loosely. Don't use adhesive. Don't break blisters, and don't apply creams, ointments, greases, butter, jellies, or antiseptics. Consult the baby's doctor for the next step.

In the case of a chemical burn, wash the area thoroughly with water—lots of water. Hold the baby under the cold faucet or a hose if necessary. Then take off any clothes and continue to pour water on the skin. After you've got all the chemical washed off, call the doctor right away.

CHOKING

If the baby can still breathe, let him or her try to cough up what's causing the problem. Don't go after it, or you may make matters worse by pushing the material farther in and blocking the breathing completely. Move the baby slowly, if at all, and hold the baby face down with the head slightly lower than the body. This puts gravity to work for you.

If the baby can't breathe, hold him or her face down as in the picture. Slap the baby on the back between the shoulder blades. This should dislodge the obstruction. If it doesn't, and the baby still can't breathe, use the now famous Heimlich maneuver. Wrap your arms around the baby, place one fist against the baby's stomach, the other hand over the fist, and make a sudden sharp motion upward toward the chest and under the breastbone. It's best if this procedure is done by someone who knows how, because done wrong it can cause harm. However, if your child is choking to death, there's no time to be choosy.

If the baby still doesn't breathe when you get the obstruction out, begin artificial respiration right away. If you are alone, tend to your baby. Don't waste time. If someone is with you, have that person call the doctor while you take care of the baby.

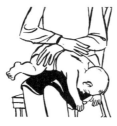

CONVULSIONS

If your baby has a seizure (convulsions), here's what to do.

(1) Put the baby on his or her abdomen or side on a surface where the thrashing about won't cause injury. A carpet will do nicely. A bed is O.K. as long as you make sure the baby doesn't fall off the edge.

(2) If you can, loosen the baby's clothing, especially anything around the neck.

(3) Look at a clock to note the time. Observe carefully what is happening so you will be able to describe it to the doctor.

(4) Let the seizure carry on as it will, and don't try to hold the baby still. When it's over, put the baby on his or her side, with the head slightly lower than the rest of the body.

(5) At no time during or right after a convulsion should you give the baby anything by mouth. Don't try to force the jaws apart or use any object to hold the mouth open.

(6) If the seizure lasts longer than 15–20 minutes, get help and proceed to the nearest hospital as fast as you can. Prolonged seizures (45–60 minutes) may result in lasting damage.

If you are alone, tend to your baby first and call the doctor as soon as the seizure has passed. If someone is with you, have that person call the doctor while you take care of the baby.

FALLS

If your baby is accidentally dropped or falls off a bed or other surface, chances are you'll go into instant panic and wonder how you could have been stupid enough to let it happen. In most cases, the baby will land head first, yet be more surprised and frightened than hurt. If nothing seems seriously wrong, and the baby stops crying within a few minutes, everything is probably fine.

Be alert for symptoms of head injury. If the baby loses consciousness, begins to vomit, has trouble breathing, becomes pale, bleeds from the ears, nose, or mouth, or shows lack of eye response or one pupil appears noticeably larger than the other, a possible problem may be indicated. If any one of these symptoms occurs following a fall, see the doctor immediately.

If the baby refuses two or more feedings or seems unusually sleepy, call the doctor. Watch the way the baby moves, and if he or she avoids moving one or more extremities, check this out with the doctor.

Be especially alert for the above-mentioned symptoms during the week to ten days following a fall.

ACCIDENTS (Prevention)

Falls, suffocation, swallowing harmful things, and automobile mishaps are the kinds of accidents most likely to harm a small baby. The suggestions that follow are not meant to alarm you, but to point out that common sense and a little extra care can keep many accidents from happening.

DON'T LET YOUR BABY CHOKE OR SUFFOCATE

(1) Never leave any kind of pliable plastic—bags or food wrap—within your baby's reach or where it could fall near the baby. Don't use plastic bags or wrap to cover mattresses or pillows.

(2) Make sure that your heating system is safe and working well. When using a gas or other space heater, leave a window in the baby's room partly open so that fresh air can get in.

(3) Keep strings and other things that could choke your baby completely away from him or her.

(a) Never tie a baby into a crib or carriage. Use a harness designed for that purpose when your baby is strong enough to climb out.
(b) Avoid baby clothes that tie shut. Snaps, zippers, and buttons are safer.
(c) Don't have window shade, venetian blind, or drapery cords within reach of the baby.

PREVENT FALLS

(1) Never leave your baby unattended on a surface from which he or she could fall. Even a newborn baby may surprise you and roll or slither to the edge.

(2) Hold on to your baby firmly when you are bathing, dressing, or changing him or her.

(3) Clutter on the stairs or floor could cause you to trip while carrying your baby. Try to keep walkways clear (not always so easy if you have other children). Hold the baby in one arm and use the other to hold the railing when going up or down stairs.

KEEP HARMFUL OBJECTS AWAY FROM BABY

(1) Your baby can't try to swallow what he or she can't reach. Keep all mouth-sized or smaller objects—beads, coins, needles and pins, pills, nuts, raisins, scissors, etc.—where your baby can't get them.

(2) If you use cloth diapers and pins, make sure you put the same number of pins into the clean diaper as you just took out of the dirty one.

(3) Make sure that heavy or sharp objects are stored where they won't be knocked over and fall on baby.

(4) Keep your baby safe from family pets (see page 66).

(5) Make sure an older child does not place harmful objects within the baby's reach.

> **Never leave your new baby alone**
> **in the house even for a few minutes.**
> **If something should go wrong,**
> **by the time you get back**
> **it might be too late.**

See Automobile Safety (below) and Car Restraints (page 46) for ways to keep your baby from injuries in a car.

AIR QUALITY

While your baby is growing up, there will be many influences in the environment that you won't be able to control. What you can do, however, is make *your* home as healthful a place to be as possible.

One of the best things you can do for your baby's immature respiratory system is to provide an atmosphere of clean air. A newborn's lungs are still developing and growing. If you or anyone else in your family smokes, don't do it in the presence of your baby. And keep the baby out of rooms where people have just been smoking. (It makes no sense to smoke in a room without the child, and then get him or her to join you in the smoke-filled room as soon as you're done.) Wood stoves, coal stoves, and other space heaters should be functioning well, with clean chimneys, and it's important to maintain a continuous source of fresh air. If improperly operated, these devices can be as harmful as tobacco smoking.

A number of studies now indicate an increased incidence of respiratory infections in children whose parents smoke. Little lungs will develop better without the stress of a smoky environment.

AUTOMOBILE SAFETY

To keep your new baby safe in an automobile, an approved infant carrier is a *must,* right from the start. Begin with the ride home from the hospital. Don't risk even one short ride in the car without the right restraint system to protect your baby. Why is this so important? Each year in the United States, automobile accidents injure approximately 150,000 children under the age of five. About 1,000 of these children die and others are severely impaired for life. Many of them would have been safe if they had been correctly buckled in.

Even if a car is not involved in a collision, an unprotected infant could be seriously hurt or killed. A sudden stop, swerve, or sharp turn could send an unrestrained infant flying. But don't hold your baby with a car's regular shoulder or lap belts. Internal injuries could result. Your arms aren't a safe place for your baby in a moving car either. If something goes wrong, you might not be able to hold onto the child. And if you do hold on, your grasp could cause harm. In a crash, a small baby could be crushed between your body and your arms, or a part of the car. The *only* safe way for your baby to travel in an automobile is in an approved infant car carrier. (See page 46.) Car beds, widely used in the 1950s, are not safe.

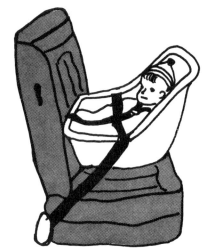

Use the infant car carrier for your baby every time you go out in the car. Be sure the straps are fastened correctly. Don't take shortcuts such as tying the belt loosely around the baby's middle. Using the carrier carelessly defeats its safety features.

Loose objects carried in the car could hurt your baby. Be sure to keep the back window ledge and dashboard clear so that nothing can bounce off and hit your baby.

BABYPROOFING

Babyproofing your home for a newborn is easy. The real fun starts later when your baby begins to crawl, walk, and grab for everything in sight.

For a new baby, just make sure that nothing harmful can fall on the baby or find its way into the crib where the baby might get it. Anything that should not go in the baby's mouth must be kept out of reach. This is simple for a baby who is not yet mobile.

Never leave plastic bags anywhere near the baby. Don't ever use plastic bags or wrap as a mattress cover or pillow case. Keep strings or anything else that could choke a child away from your baby. Make sure that your baby's toys don't have any removable or glued-on parts that could come off and be swallowed. Watch out for eyes on stuffed animals. Even a newborn may attempt to remove them. If you have an older child, babyproofing requires that the older child not have unsupervised access to objects that could be a danger to the baby.

If you have pets in your home, be careful not to leave your newborn baby where an animal could accidentally harm him or her. (See page 66.)

BABYSITTERS

Finding a good babysitter for a newborn baby can be a very difficult task. If you're going to use a sitter, it's best to make arrangements ahead of time. How you go about this will, of course, depend on where you live, your lifestyle, and what your needs are.

For the first month or six weeks, it's probably best if you take care of your baby yourself as much as you can. Of course, if you have to return to work, this isn't always possible. Try taking the baby with you when you go visiting or to a restaurant. This is often far better than worrying about leaving your baby with someone.

There really aren't any firm rules for selecting a good babysitter. You have to do what makes sense for you. Here are some suggestions.

• If your baby is lucky enough to have grandparents who are willing and able to help, this may be a good choice for the early days.

• Don't leave a newborn with a very young or inexperienced teen-ager. It's not fair to either of them.

• Sources of babysitters include recommendations from friends, local church or community groups, your doctor, or other professionals who might be helpful.

• Interview before you hire. The person who worked perfectly for your best friend's child might be a disaster in your home.

• Make very clear just what you expect your babysitter to do. If you are not there, then the primary responsibility involves keeping your baby comfortable and safe. Don't expect a childcare expert, housecleaner, laundress, and maintenance engineer all rolled into one.

• Try having the babysitter take care of your child when you are home for a short time. You can tell a lot this way. If things go well, you'll feel better about leaving your baby when you need to go out.

• Be sure to provide whatever emergency information is necessary. Make sure the sitter knows what to do and whom to call if something goes wrong.

• If you're not happy about a childcare arrangement you've made, change it. Remember, it's *your* baby and *your* responsibility.

BATHS

Bathing your baby can be fun. You don't need to make a big production out of it. Don't be scared off by the long lists of rules you find in some books. If the formal bath demonstration at the hospital intimidated you, forget that too. Just use common sense and some soap and water. No matter how well prepared, some parents are still terrified by the thought of bathing a newborn baby. If you feel that way, here are some things to remember.

• Your baby is a lot smaller than you are. You'll manage to hold on even if he or she protests.

• Water won't make your baby dissolve.

• Baths need not be long.

• If you can't cope with giving your baby a tub bath when you first get home from the hospital, don't worry. You'll feel more secure as time goes on. Until then, just be sure to keep the diaper area clean, and wash any milk out of the folds in the baby's neck.

SPONGE BATHS

You should stick to sponge baths until your baby's navel has healed. And a sponge bath will do nicely any time you don't feel like bothering with a tub bath. Here are some things to remember.

• Use warm water. (Test it with your elbow. If it feels barely warm, not hot, it's fine.)

• Use any mild, neutral soap that won't burn the eyes. Dial or Ivory are examples of soaps that are suitable for use with newborns. Special baby soaps are best. Skip expensive toilet soaps because the perfume may irritate baby's skin. Save these for yourself.

• Use a washcloth or a little bath sponge. Or you can lather the baby with your hands. Do whatever works for you. Rinse very thoroughly and then dry.

• If you wish, you can wash your baby one part at a time, dry, reclothe it, and then go on to the next part. If the room is cool, your baby is less likely to get chilled this way.

• Be sure to do all the creases. Dry them carefully when you're done.

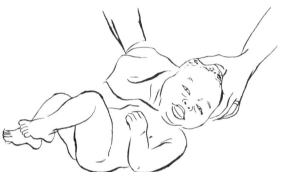

• Plain water will do on the face. To clean the eyes, wipe quickly with a wet, clean cloth. Wipe from the nose out. Use a fresh corner of the cloth for the other eye. Cotton balls may leave lint in or around the eyes, so a cloth is safer.

• To clean the baby's ears and nose, wash gently whatever you can see. Don't poke Q-Tips up into the nostrils or the ears.

• Until the baby's navel has healed, clean around and under the umbilical stump with alcohol on a Q-Tip after each bath. This promotes drying.

TUB BATHS

As soon as the baby's navel has healed, you can begin the fun of a tub bath if you wish.

• A plastic dishpan is excellent. When your baby is still small, any container that's clean and handy will do fine.

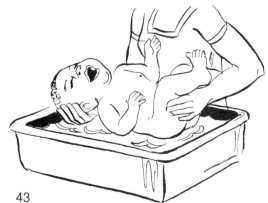

• Use warm, not hot, water. Never put your baby under the faucet or let water run into the tub while the baby is in it. A temperature change may occur and harm your baby.

43

- Get everything you need before you put your baby into the water. *Never* leave your baby alone in water even for a few seconds. A baby can drown in an inch of water or less.

- Hold the baby firmly in whatever way is comfortable for both of you. Wash and rinse the different parts just the way you did for a sponge bath.

- Take the baby out and dry carefully. You're done!

SHAMPOOS

If you plan to wash your baby's head, you can do this either as part of a tub bath or a sponge bath.

- Wet and lather well. Keep the soap out of baby's eyes. If you use a baby shampoo, it won't feel quite as bad when you do get a drop in an eye by mistake.

- Rinse carefully. Use a wet cloth or sponge, or you can pour water back over a baby's head from a plastic cup or other container. Never let water from the faucet run onto your baby. You may find it easiest to hold the baby in the "football" position as you rinse.

- Dry as thoroughly as you can with a soft towel.

BOOKS

Begin to share books with your baby right away. Even a newborn will enjoy the sound of your voice as you read. This is true long before he or she can understand the story or the pictures. See pages 85–87 for specific suggestions on reading to your new baby and books you both might enjoy.

BOWEL MOVEMENTS

A baby's first bowel movement is made up of a sticky, smooth material called meconium. The color of a meconium movement is generally a dark greenish-black. If a new baby does not have this first bowel movement within 36 hours of birth, the doctor should be consulted.

The frequency of normal bowel movements can vary greatly from one baby to another. For breast-fed babies, an average of three to six stools a day is usual, although some babies may comfortably go several days between bowel movements. The stools of breast-fed babies are generally yellowish in color. They are usually like loose cottage cheese in texture, with a sweet-sour odor.

The stools of bottle-fed babies are generally pasty and firmer than those of breast-fed babies. Their color ranges from pale yellow to dark tan, and the odor may be quite strong. Bottle-fed babies have fewer movements—one to four per day at first.

During the first few weeks, you'll have changed enough diapers to become quite familiar with what a normal stool is for your baby. Some variation from one movement to the next is, of course, quite normal. A very marked change in color or consistency, without a change in diet, could be a cause for concern. Call your baby's doctor if the problem persists.

BREATHING

The breathing of newborn babies is often noisy. They cough and sneeze frequently. Many babies snore. This is usually no cause for concern. The nasal passages of a newborn baby are very narrow. Even a tiny speck of dust or dried mucus may be enough to set off a sneeze. Noisy breathing is often caused by excessive vibration of immature vocal cords as the baby inhales. Although the gasping that results may sound alarming, it's not usually a problem.

New parents often worry about the shallow, seemingly irregular breathing that is common and normal for many new babies. You may find yourself checking frequently to see if your sleeping baby is still breathing. Lots of parents do this and are reassured when they find that all is well. You should check with your baby's doctor, however, if you are at all concerned about the way your baby breathes—if, for example, you feel that the pauses are too long or the pattern is too irregular. If your baby should stop breathing, see page 36 for what to do until medical help arrives.

BURPING AND BUBBLES

Babies swallow air along with their milk and when they cry. It's important to help your baby burp up the air bubbles at these times. Here are two ways you can burp your baby.

(1) Hold the baby up against your chest so the baby is looking out over your shoulder. Rub or pat the baby's back gently. (Don't pound!) Put a diaper over your shoulder in case milk comes up with the bubble.

(2) Hold the baby in a sitting position in your lap. Support the chin with one hand. Gently rub the back with the other.

If no bubbles come up in two or three minutes, put the baby down on his or her tummy for a minute or two. Then pick up the baby and try again. If still no bubble and the baby is happy, go on with the meal. At times your baby just might not be bothered by bubbles.

At first, try burping a bottle-fed baby after each ounce of formula. Burp a breast-fed baby between breasts and when the feeding is over. You'll soon figure out what's best for your baby. Some babies stop sucking when they need to be burped. Others don't. You'll soon get to know your child. Don't skip the bubble step. If you do, a bubble might come up on its own later and bring the entire feeding with it.

CAR BEDS

Despite its name, never use an infant car bed to carry your child in a moving vehicle. It will not protect your baby. Only an approved car restraint will do that job properly. (See page 40.) A baby doesn't need a car bed for sleeping, even on long trips. Most babies sleep very well in the semi-sitting position of an infant car seat. Small receiving blankets or rolled diapers tucked between the sides of the carrier and a baby's head will keep even the tiniest baby comfortably centered in the seat. Another trick is to put a folded receiving blanket under the baby's buttocks so that the knees can bend slightly.

If you have a car bed, you will find many uses for it in places other than the car. Use it as a portable crib in the house, and your baby can join you in any room. When you take your baby visiting, he or she can sleep in the car bed. A car bed is not something you need to run out and buy. The cardboard container many hospitals use for newborns serves as an excellent portable crib for the first month or so.

CAR RESTRAINTS

In a car carrier designed for newborns, a safety harness keeps your baby in place as he or she reclines in a deep, shell-like seat. The car's seat belt secures the entire device—baby and all—to the car. In such a carrier, your baby can safely ride in either the front or the back seat of the car, whichever you prefer. Wherever the baby rides, however, be sure to place the carrier so that the baby is facing the rear of the car.

Which infant car carrier should you use? Pick one that has been dynamically tested (crash tested) and meets current safety standards. Federal guidelines for infant and car restraints were updated in 1981. The new specifications were designed to make the restraints safer and easier to use. Read the label carefully before you buy. If the seat meets current regulations, it will say so on the box. For your new baby, be sure you use a carrier designed for infants, not one that's only for older children. Some infant carriers will be fine until your baby weighs 20 pounds, which will get you through much of the first year. Others can be used in different positions to accommodate newborns, infants, and toddlers up to 40 pounds. Make sure that the carrier you select fits in your car. Your car's seat belts must be long enough to stretch across the carrier and fasten easily.

To find out more about infant and child car seats, get the pamphlet called "Don't Risk Your Child's Life," published by Physicians for Automotive Safety. Send 35¢ and a stamped, self-addressed envelope to **Physicians for Automotive Safety**, 50 Union Avenue, Irvington, N.J. 17111. It contains useful information about available products, along with brand names and model numbers of safe car seats. This pamphlet is revised frequently and is an excellent source of up-to-date information.

If the cost of a new infant car carrier is a problem for you, try borrowing one from a friend whose child has outgrown it. Used ones can often be found at garage or yard sales. In many areas, infant carriers can be rented for a very low fee. Ask your doctor or local baby clinic. No matter how you get one, however, an approved infant car seat is one item you can't afford to skip if you plan to take your baby anywhere in an automobile.

CARRIAGES AND STROLLERS

A carriage—especially the elegant type that looks a bit like Cinderella's coach —is probably not a cost-effective investment. Large carriages are expensive. They also require storage room and places to use them. They don't do well in crowded supermarkets, small elevators, or places with lots of stairs.

An umbrella stroller designed to hold an infant car seat would probably be a more practical choice for many families. Even a tiny baby can roll happily along in one of these while secured in the car seat. You can take it anywhere in the car. And, when your baby is bigger and able to sit up, you can convert the stroller to use without the car seat.

If, however, you feel that a traditional baby carriage or pram is a luxury you wish to have, here are some things to look for and questions to ask before you buy.

(1) Is the carriage sturdy enough to be strong but light enough to manage?

(2) Is it deep enough to be safe? Is the inside well lined? Is the lining safely secured? (Avoid linings attached with brads or other decorative bits of hardware which might come loose and be swallowed.)

(3) Do the brakes work easily? Will they hold well enough?

(4) Is there a place to attach a harness? Your baby will be sitting and standing before you know it.

(5) Can you push the carriage easily? Is the handle at a comfortable height for you?

(6) If the top part is designed to be removed for use as a portable crib, does it work easily? Does it fasten back on securely? Although this feature will make it easy to transport the carriage in your car, remember that a carriage top on the back seat is not a safe car restraint for your baby.

(7) Do you really like the carriage? Be sure, before you buy it.

CARRIER (Basket)

A basket carrier—available with bright paisley lining—is a lovely luxury for carrying a newborn baby. In this type of basket, a tiny baby is as easy to carry as a briefcase. When you get to where you're going, the basket serves as an attractive little bed as well as a great conversation piece.

A basket carrier, like a front pack, is something that suits some mothers and not others. It depends on your lifestyle and personal preference. It's great for taking a newborn baby to meetings, restaurants, church, work, or to visit friends. It fits easily in the trunk of a car. When you get where you're going, you can take your baby out of the car restraint and put him or her into the basket.

The basket carrier shown here can be ordered from

Growing & Learning Co.
5007 River Road, PO Box 4190
New Orleans, LA 70178

A basket carrier is expensive and your baby will outgrow it in three or four months. At this point it becomes a costly bed for dolls or stuffed animals. If you really want to splurge, a tiny matching version for a small doll is also available.

CARRIER (Soft Front Pack)

Many mothers find a soft front pack carrier (such as Snugli) to be very handy for carrying a new baby. You can keep the baby near you and still have both hands free for whatever you're doing. Baby can rest securely and comfortably while listening to your heartbeat and breathing. Certain carriers are designed so that your baby can nurse while being carried.

If you think a front carrier would be helpful for you, try one before you buy. It may suit you very well. Some mothers say they couldn't manage without one. Others don't find this type of carrier to be as wonderful as they had hoped. It's really a matter of personal preference.

The carrier you buy should be sturdy and well made. It should be washable. Make sure that you can put it on without help.

CHANGING THE BABY

Even if you've never changed a baby before, you'll become an expert very quickly. Your baby will see to that. Just do it. You and your baby will work out a routine that is comfortable for both of you. All you have to do is get the wet diaper off, clean the baby's bottom, and put the clean diaper on.

Here are a few hints to make changing time easier for both of you.

• Make sure everything you need is within reach before you begin to change your baby. (You'll see how important this is the first time you open a badly soiled diaper and have nothing handy to clean the baby's bottom.)

• If you've disregarded Step 1, and do need something, don't leave your baby unattended on a surface from which he or she could fall. Reapply the soiled diaper and take the baby with you to get what you need.

• Many babies wet again right in the middle of the changing process. They almost seem to plan it that way, so be prepared. Shield a little boy's penis with the diaper you've just removed until you're ready to fasten the new one. This will keep you from being sprayed in the face as you bend over your baby. Or, if you have a little girl, put an extra cloth diaper or a waterproof pad under her to catch the puddle.

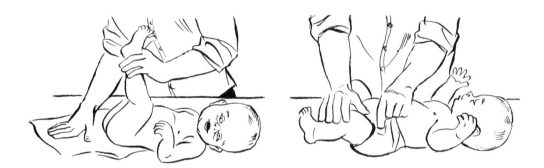

• Although they are costly, disposable diaper wipes are handy for keeping baby's bottom clean. (Buy the jumbo size containers. Make your own travel packs by putting a few wipes in a pantyhose container. You can save quite a bit this way.)

• An economical alternative to the packaged disposable wipes is a roll of paper towels and a squeeze bottle of plain water.

• If you use cloth diapers, sticking the pins into a bar of soap from time to time will make it easier to get them into the diaper. (Keeping the paper wrapper on the soap prevents the cake from flaking apart when you stick pins in it.)

• When you push a pin into your baby's diaper, put your other hand behind where you're pushing the pin. This way you'll stick yourself, not your baby, if you complete the task too vigorously.

• The diaper should be tight enough around the baby's legs to prevent large-scale leaks. But be careful that it's not too tight. You don't want it to bind or irritate the baby either.

• If you use disposable diapers, don't get anything (oil, powder, lotion, etc.) on the tapes or the diaper area to which the tapes adhere. Only clean tapes stick well. Keep a roll of masking tape handy to deal with diaper tapes that don't hold.

• If you don't get the diaper just perfect, leave it as long as it's not hurting the baby. You'll have a chance to change it again very soon.

CIRCUMCISION CARE

If you have your baby boy circumcised, it will take a week or two until the sensitive area is completely healed. To protect the unhealed circumcision, place generous amounts of Vaseline on a piece of sterile gauze and wrap this loosely around the tip of the baby's penis. Doing this at each diaper change will keep the diaper from sticking to the baby and adding to his discomfort. You'll probably find a tube of Vaseline easiest to use for this. You'll get just the right amount and none on your hands. For maximum safety, invest in a new container of Vaseline. An open jar lying around the house just won't do.

If the baby's penis bleeds or becomes swollen, consult your pediatrician.

CLOTHING

Where you live, what time of year your baby is born, and your own personal preference will help you decide what your baby should wear. Here are some basic points about clothing your child.

• Your baby is going to grow very quickly, so garments in the newborn size will be short-lived. Items in the six-month size can be used for most babies even at the start, and these will last longer.

• Don't overdress your child. A comfortable baby, not an overheated one is your goal. Use common sense and your own comfort as your guide. If you need a sweater, your baby probably will too. If you're very warm, a diaper and perhaps a shirt will be all the baby will require.

• Babies aren't usually very neat. They spit, spill, soil, and wet. Pick clothes that launder easily.

• In very warm weather, stay away from synthetic fabrics which block air circulation and function like little ovens.

• Select garments that are easy to put on and off your baby. You need to be able to get to the diaper area easily. You don't want to disrobe your baby entirely just to change a diaper. Shirts which wrap around and snap shut are easier to use than the ones you must pull over the baby's head.

• Flame-retardant fabric should be used in all children's sleepwear. Tris, a substance used in the past to treat fabrics, was suspected of causing cancer, and was banned in 1977 by the U.S. Consumer Product Safety Commission. Some companies illegally continued the distribution of Tris-treated fabrics. As recently as the summer of 1981, some stores were still known to be selling Tris-treated garments. To be on the safe side, read the labels carefully before you buy. Stay away from fabrics containing acetate, triacetate, or blends of these fabrics. Don't risk buying your baby a bargain-priced garment without the label. You could be buying trouble instead.

• Before you buy a large number of any particular garment, try one to see if the style suits you and your baby. Some mothers, for example, find little nightgowns with drawstring bottoms to be very handy for a sleeping baby. Others find the tying and untying to be very inconvenient (sometimes impossible), and much prefer to let the baby wear stretch jumpsuits with feet. The use of the jumpsuits makes booties (which come off and get lost) unnecessary.

• Bright colors and variety will appeal to both you and your baby. There's no rule that says you must stick to pink or blue.

• Quantities of some items will depend on how you do the laundry. A washer and dryer in the home, or household help to assist you, will enable you to manage with smaller quantities than if you must personally take the laundry out to a laundromat once a week.

COLIC

What is colic? Colic is a severe bellyache and crying spell for your baby. It can also mean a severe headache and perhaps a crying spell for you too. Some babies go through infancy without a sign of colic. Others are severely afflicted on a daily basis for as long as several weeks.

We're not really sure why some babies become colicky and others do not. Some people blame the condition on nervous mothers. This is not fair. A tendency for colic just seems to be built into the temperament of certain children. One baby in a family may have it. Another may not.

If a baby is going to be colicky, the problem is most likely to occur between three and eight weeks of age. How can you cope with a colicky baby? Here are some hints on handling the problem. Use whatever works for you. If nothing works, try to keep calm and be reassured that these trials will pass. By the fourth month, as baby's digestive system becomes more mature, the worst of colic will be over.

• Hold the baby securely in your arms and pace the floor. Being walked often helps baby to feel better. This technique also gives you something to do besides worry.

• Check again for a wet or dirty diaper. Changing the baby may provide some diversion for you both.

• Offer a bit of warm water in a bottle. Some babies find this soothing.

• Use a warm (not too hot) hot water bottle on the baby's back or abdomen.

• Try swaddling your baby. (See page 71.)

• If this suggestion appeals to you, check it out with your pediatrician first. Try a tiny bit of a sweet-tasting liqueur such as Irish Cream, Kahlua, Vandermint, or Creme de Menthe. This also works for teething discomforts later on. Pick a flavor you like. If it doesn't work for your baby, at least you'll feel better.

- Keep trying to get the bubbles up.

- Hold the baby, sit in a rocking chair, and rock. You'll both benefit.

- The basket carrier described on page 47 can be swung or rocked back and forth. Your baby may find this soothing.

- Music diverts some babies from their discomfort.

- If you have an infant swing, try it for the baby.

- Put your baby into the infant car carrier, get in the car, and take a ride. The motion and sounds of a car will usually calm a colicky baby.

If all else fails, you may just need to let the baby cry it out for a while. You'll all feel bad about this approach, but it may be the only way, Don't be afraid to ask your pediatrician for help in dealing with a colicky baby.

CONSTIPATION

Constipation is seldom a problem in a newborn baby, especially one who is breast-fed. Some anxious mothers, however, worry that a day without a soiled diaper indicates trouble. Be reassured that the normal frequency of bowel movements can vary greatly from one baby to another. Some babies pass several stools a day. Others may comfortably space their bowel movements several days apart. Such infrequent bowel movements are not a sign of constipation or cause for concern as long as the stools are reasonably soft when they are passed.

If your baby does pass small, rabbit-pellet type of stools, this indicates constipation. In most cases, this situation can be corrected by giving dark Karo syrup (1 teaspoon to 4 ounces of water) once or twice a day. Check with your baby's doctor first.

If your baby appears very uncomfortable or appears to be straining too much with a bowel movement, stimulation with a rectal thermometer may help.

CRADLE CAP

Cradle cap is a scaly crust often found on a baby's head. It may be yellowish or simply dirty in appearance. It is an accumulation of dried oil from the many tiny oil glands in the scalp holding down the surface material normally shed by the skin. Although cradle cap isn't a serious health problem, it can become one, and it doesn't look very nice. Deal with it before it gets out of control.

When you wash the baby's head using mild soap or baby shampoo, rub vigorously with fingertips or a terrycloth washrag to loosen and remove the scales. Don't be afraid to rub the soft spot. If this doesn't take care of the cradle cap, you can apply warm baby oil or a bit of Vaseline to the baby's scalp. One to two hours later, when the scales have softened, remove as many as you can with a fine-toothed comb. Then shampoo. Frequent brushing with a very soft bristled brush may help, even if your baby doesn't have very much hair.

If your baby's scalp becomes red and/or weepy (oozing), or for very severe cases of cradle cap that don't seem to respond to the above treatment, consult your baby's doctor.

CRIB BUMPERS

Crib bumpers keep your sleeping baby's hands and feet inside the crib. They provide a comfortable cushion. And perhaps most important of all for a newborn, they keep your baby out of drafts.

A bumper should fit well and tie or snap securely. It must attach to the crib in at least six places so that it will stay where it belongs and your baby won't dislodge it or get caught in it. Be sure to check from time to time to make sure that the fasteners or ties are firm. Some babies manage to find them to chew on, and this could be a danger.

CRIB DEATH

The subject of Crib Death (Sudden Infant Death Syndrome) has received considerable attention in the media recently. Although the chances are very, very slight (there are roughly 2 cases for 1,000 live births) that you would ever be faced with this problem directly, you should know some of the facts about it.

Crib death is the sudden and unexpected death of a well or almost well infant, and the reasons for its happening remain unexplained even after an autopsy. Most crib deaths occur among infants 2 to 4 months of age, and few infants over 6 months are involved.

Some "near-miss" babies narrowly escape becoming victims of this mysterious malady because someone just happens to be there when the baby stops breathing. If you should see your baby stop breathing and begin turning blue for no apparent reason, begin artificial respiration (mouth-to-mouth breathing) immediately. (See page 36.) Tactile stimulation—holding and touching the baby—may also help.

Report any occurrence of such a "near miss" to your baby's pediatrician immediately. Babies who are known to be at risk can be placed on monitors that warn when there is any interruption of breathing or heartbeat. Most victims of crib death, however, give no advance indication of any problem. The parents of such a child must understand that they have not been negligent, and their sad loss does not imply guilt on their part.

CRIBS

What should your baby sleep in? In the first few weeks, when your baby is very small, there are many possibilities. (See page 58 for suggestions about temporary sleeping containers.) If you plan to buy a crib right away for your newborn, here are some safety features to keep in mind. (New cribs are required by law to have these essential safety features. These points are especially important to keep in mind if you are buying a secondhand crib or borrowing one from a friend.)

- The slats should be no farther apart than 2-3/8″ so that the baby's head can't get caught.

- That mattress should fit tightly, with no room for the baby to squeeze between it and the sides.

• Surfaces should be nontoxic, and splinter free.

• Hardware should be safe and secure. There shouldn't be any sharp parts, things that could break off, or movable features that move when they're not supposed to.

• Decorative features, if any, must be safe. There should be nothing that could catch or injure the baby.

If you plan to put the crib against a wall, only one side of the crib needs to drop down. (These may be slightly less expensive.)

CRYING

Newborn babies cry because they need something. You may not always know what that something is, but you should try to figure it out. Don't worry about spoiling your new baby. You won't. Letting a baby cry does not build character. What it may do, however, is communicate to your baby that you don't care.

Attend to your crying baby promptly. This will help him or her to feel loved and secure. Prompt attention does not reinforce the crying. As a matter of fact, babies whose needs are met quickly tend to cry less often and for shorter periods of time.

Many mothers seem to be able to tell a "wet cry" from a "hungry cry" or a "bubble cry" with uncanny accuracy. Don't be upset if you can't. Some babies are easy to figure out right from the start. Others aren't. Just do the best you can. Here are some questions to help you figure out why your baby is crying.

(1) Is your baby hungry or thirsty?

(2) Does your baby's diaper need changing?

(3) Does your baby need to suck?

(4) Does your baby need to be burped?

(5) Does your baby need to sleep?

(6) Is your baby startled? To break the startle cycle, pick the baby up and hold him or her securely. Or leave the baby lying down and firmly hold one of your baby's legs or arms. This seems to work.

(7) Is your baby uncomfortable? Too hot or too cold? Is something pinching or irritating? Has the baby been in one position for too long?

(8) Some or all of the above? Sometimes you'll need to fix more than one discomfort before your baby settles down. Try different things in whatever order makes sense to you.

(9) None of the above? This is the tough one. Occasionally you won't be able to figure out why your baby is crying. Walk around holding the baby close to your body. At least let your baby sense that you're trying. In the long run these efforts will pay off.

DIAPERS (Choices)

Disposable diapers are expensive. They are also very convenient and easy to use. Whether to use them all of the time, some of the time, or not at all is a personal choice you will have to make. Here are some things to think about:

• Some people avoid disposable diapers for ecological reasons. (The plastic parts are not biodegradable and the paper parts are made from trees.) But before you decide against disposables on this account, remember that laundering of cloth diapers adds detergent wastes to the environment and that a washer and dryer consume energy.

• Cloth diapers are cheaper than disposables. This may not be so, however, if you add in reasonable compensation for your time and effort as well as the other costs of doing laundry, such as detergent, hot water, electricity, etc.

We found disposable diapers to be so much more convenient, that the costs—both economic and ecological—seemed justified in the total picture. Think over the issues involved, and make whatever decision you feel is best.

DIAPERS (Cloth)

If you decide to use cloth diapers, you'll need at least 4 to 5 dozen of them. You'll want more if you have to take your laundry out to a commercial laundromat. You may be able to do with a dozen less if you have a washer and dryer right in your house or apartment. Even if you plan to use disposables, you should have a dozen cloth diapers on hand. They make excellent bibs and mops, as well as being a handy backup for those times you run out of disposables and can't get to the store. (If, of course, you also have diaper pins at home.)

Cloth diapers come in several different types of cloth and shapes. Prefolded diapers have extra thickness already located where it is needed, but some prefolded types will require additional folding to fit the tiny bottom of a newborn. Shop around until you find the kind that makes the most sense to you. You might decide to start with a dozen or two and some boxes of disposables for the first week or so until you are sure you have made the right choice for you.

There are several ways you can fold a cloth diaper. Try them out and pick the one that's easiest for you and fits your baby best.

You needn't bother to fold a diaper until it's time to use it. (Unless, of course, you feel a need for clean, neat piles of laundry.) Just keep diapers stored in the laundry basket as they come out of the dryer. Fold them one at a time as you're changing the baby. This way you won't waste time folding the many diapers you'll use for bibs or mops.

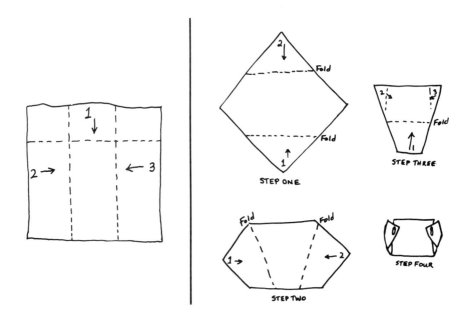

DIAPERS (Disposable)

If you decide to use disposable diapers, try different brands until you find out what works best for you and your baby. Some babies are sensitive to the perfumed deodorant used in certain brands of disposables. If so, you'll have to switch.

Here are some ways to keep the cost of disposables down. Be sure to get the samples offered in many hospital gift packs. Be on the lookout for discount coupons in newspapers and magazines. Buy the larger convenience packs or cases rather than the single small boxes. Shop for price. You'll be surprised at the variation. When you change your baby, keep a roll of masking tape handy to reseal a dry diaper opened by mistake or to repair a defective tape. Be sure to use the right size diaper for your new baby. The larger ones are more expensive.

For greater absorbancy (during the night or any other time) you can use two disposables at once. Just cut a hole in the plastic cover of the diaper you will put closest to the baby. Then the outer diaper will be able to draw away and absorb as much liquid as possible.

Be sure to change disposable diapers often enough. Your baby can be very wet in a disposable diaper and the plastic cover may conceal this. Leaving a baby wet too long can contribute to diaper rash. So, even if your baby doesn't complain about being wet, it's best to change the diaper when needed.

DIAPER RASH

Diaper rash is often a problem for newborn babies with sensitive skin. To help prevent diaper rash, change your baby frequently and wash his or her bottom at *every* change. If your baby shows signs of diaper rash, here are some things that might help.

- Clean the diaper area with water or disposable wipes after every change. Do this even if the diaper is wet rather than soiled. (The ammonia left by the urine can be extremely irritating to your baby's tender skin even if the baby looks clean.)

- Change your baby's diaper more often. This is especially important if you use disposable diapers which can hold a lot of irritating moisture without seeming to be wet.

- If you use cloth diapers, skip the rubber pants for a while. Use two diapers at once to prevent leaks.

- If you can, try letting the baby go without any diaper at all for a while. Exposure to air helps stop the rash. Put several layers of diaper and a rubber pad under the baby to protect the crib.

- If your location and the time of year permit, a little sunshine and fresh air can be a help. But be careful not to trade your baby's diaper rash for a sunburned bottom!

- An ointment such as Vaseline, A & D, Desitin, or Diaperene may help protect your baby's bottom from diaper rash and give healing a chance to start if a rash has started. Zinc oxide ointment is inexpensive and effective.

- If you use cloth diapers, make sure that they are well rinsed so no soap remains. Changing brands of detergent or using a liquid detergent may help. Raise the temperature of the wash water if possible. A softener might help. A cup of white vinegar in the rinse water will neutralize traces of ammonia from the baby's urine. After laundering diapers, you can boil them for ten minutes or so in a great big pot of water. This is an extra precaution to make sure that the irritants have been removed. In good weather, sun drying and bleaching are the best possible neutralizers. If cloth diapers still appear soiled or grayish after careful laundering, it's all right to use bleach. Be sure to rinse very thoroughly. Stained diapers definitely seem to increase the risk of getting a persistent diaper rash.

If you've tried these suggestions for two or three days and your baby has a severe diaper rash which does not seem to respond to treatment, consult your physician.

DIARRHEA

Diarrhea (watery stools) can be a serious problem for a newborn. Sometimes it may be difficult to tell if a baby really has a case of diarrhea or simply the frequent, loose bowel movements common to many newborns. How can you tell? A baby with diarrhea passes stools that have little or no formed material in them. They usually differ in color from normal stools. The stools may be frequent, noisy, and passed with considerable force. They may contain mucus or blood.

A baby with diarrhea can easily become dehydrated, which is a very dangerous condition for a newborn. Call your pediatrician immediately if your baby seems to have diarrhea with one or more of these other symptoms: mucus or blood in the stools, vomiting, temperature below 97.6 or above 99.6 degrees F., lack of appetite, decreased quantity of urine, decreased energy and activity level.

FEVER

The only way to tell for sure if your baby has a fever is to take his or her temperature with a thermometer. (See page 72 for directions on how to do this.) Feeling the baby's forehead is not a reliable source of information. Use of digital forehead strips is also unreliable. Use a thermometer.

If you think your baby might be sick, and you decide to call the pediatrician, you'll probably be asked what the baby's temperature is. Be prepared to answer that question by taking the temperature before you make the call (unless, of course, you are dealing with an emergency where minutes could make a difference).

A normal rectal temperature for a baby is 99.6 degrees F. (37.6 degrees C.). If you use the axillary (armpit) method, a normal temperature is 97.6 degrees F. (36.7 degrees C.). You should call the doctor if your new baby's rectal temperature is below 97.6 or above 99.6 degrees F. This is especially important if other symptoms of illness are present.

FURNITURE FOR BABY

Don't feel that you must run out and buy an expensive set of color-coordinated furniture for your baby. (Of course, if you want to and you can afford it, go right ahead. Just remember that there are lots of things more important than furniture.)

At first, all you'll really need is something for the baby to sleep in, a surface on which to change the baby, and somewhere to store clothes and supplies so that they'll be handy. It's possible for many families to meet all these needs without buying anything new in the early weeks. Here's how.

• A newborn baby can sleep in a dresser drawer (out of the dresser, of course) until you make more permanent sleeping arrangements. Pad the bottom with a folded blanket. A pillow case makes a fitted sheet, but don't put the baby on a soft pillow which could cause smothering. If your hospital uses cardboard containers for cribs, be sure to bring the baby's crib home. It's a useful, very portable sleeping container.

• You can change your baby anywhere. An elaborate changing table is not necessary. A towel spread out on any flat surface will do—a countertop, table, bed, or even the floor if your back can handle it.

• You can use any comfortable chair for holding and feeding your baby. A rocking chair is a wonderfully helpful item. It can soothe both you and your baby. If you don't have a rocking chair and can't borrow one, try garage sales or secondhand shops. You can, of course, survive without a rocking chair, but you'll find it helpful, particularly if your baby tends to be fussy.

• You can store your baby's things in cut-down cardboard boxes from a local package store. (Be careful about the source. Avoid boxes that might contain roaches or other insects.) These can be covered with bright contact paper to make them attractive.

The major point of these suggestions is simply that costly furniture doesn't make a family. A baby's room that looks like a magazine illustration may be nice, but you can be a good parent without that. So don't be intimidated by pushy salespeople or lists of things you supposedly should buy before your baby arrives.

By the time you've finished reading this book, you'll have a pretty good idea of the things you'll be doing with your new baby. In deciding what furniture you need, keep in mind your finances, life style, and available space. Get what makes sense to you.

HEAT RASH (Prickly Heat)

In hot weather, many babies get a rash called prickly heat—very tiny pink pimples and blotches and perhaps some blisters. Prickly heat usually begins around the baby's neck and shoulders. In severe cases it may spread to the rest of the baby's body. You'll probably worry about it more than it will trouble the baby, but you should take care of it promptly even if the baby doesn't appear to be bothered.

The best treatment is also the key to prevention. Keep the baby dressed appropriately for the weather. Remove the baby's clothes if the weather is very hot. A light dusting with baby powder or cornstarch might help. Take care that the baby doesn't breathe in any of the powder. Sprinkle it on your hands, and then apply it gently to the baby's skin. Don't shake it directly on the baby.

Heat rash is not only a summer problem. It is also common in winter, when babies tend to be overdressed in heated houses, cars, or stores.

HICCUPS

Babies sometimes get hiccups along with their bubbles and burps. These usually stop when the next bubble comes up, and they are generally no cause to worry. The baby is probably less bothered by them than you are. Putting the baby back to the bottle or breast to suck for a bit may help. Or you might try offering some warm water in a bottle. Placing the baby on his or her stomach sometimes helps. Or, try holding the baby upright over your shoulder with the weight and pressure on the baby's chest, not abdomen. These changes in position often make a difference.

It has been said that a tiny dab of honey or jelly on the tip of a small spoon sometimes works wonders when all else fails. However, we caution you about the use of honey (especially raw, unpasteurized honey) with a newborn, as this has been known to cause botulism, which can be very harmful, even fatal. The American Academy of Pediatrics recommends that no honey (raw or processed) be offered to a child less than a year old.

HOLDING YOUR BABY

Many new parents are a bit fearful about handling their newborn baby. Don't be afraid to hold, touch, and cuddle your child. Babies are not as fragile as they might seem, and they need to be held.

When you pick up your baby, use both hands. Support the baby's head and neck with one hand. Use the other hand to reach around and support the baby's bottom and back. Remember that your arms were designed to cradle an infant. Just do what seems most comfortable for you and the baby. Be sure to support the head and neck, and hold onto your baby firmly enough so that a sudden startle won't send the little one flying.

It's important to touch and cuddle your baby. A baby who is held firmly and gently is likely to be more secure than one who is not. However, shaking or tossing a newborn about—even in play—could cause serious harm. Handle your baby gently. Don't play rough. Don't bounce a newborn up and down to bring up the bubbles or for any other reason. Don't pound too vigorously on a baby's back as you try to burp him or her. This warning is especially important if your baby is very small and new. Premature babies are especially vulnerable.

INFANT SEATS

An infant seat is a lightweight plastic seat in which your baby can recline. A strap around the waist and between the legs keeps the baby in. Many models adjust to several positions. For a very young baby, the flattest position (fully reclined) is usually best. An older baby can sit more upright.

Infant seats are handy and inexpensive. You can use one to enable an awake baby to be with you anywhere in the house. Here are some hints for using one.

- Always keep the strap fastened. Even the tiniest baby might manage to move out of the seat.

- Don't leave your baby in a seat unattended on a table or other high surface. If you must leave the room, the infant seat is safer on the floor.

- Never use an infant seat as a car seat. It isn't sturdy enough and won't protect your baby in an accident.

- An infant seat is topheavy with baby in it. It's fine for a very young baby. For a stronger, more mobile infant, however, great care must be used. A sturdier seat would be preferable after the first four months or so.

JAUNDICE

Mild jaundice is a common condition of the newborn. Many full-term babies and an even higher percentage of those born prematurely have some degree of jaundice during the first week.

Jaundice is caused by an accumulation in the skin of a pigment called bilirubin. Bilirubin is one of the substances released when red blood cells break down. It is processed by the liver and passed out of the body in the stools.

Healthy babies are born with more red blood cells than they need, and these break down rapidly in the first few days and weeks after birth. However, a new baby's liver is immature, and the bilirubin level often builds up faster than the liver can process it. This causes jaundice.

Mild jaundice is usually no cause for concern, and in most cases it will disappear by the time the baby is six or seven days old. However, because excessive amounts of bilirubin can cause serious harm, a newborn should be watched carefully for jaundice during the first week, especially the first three days.

If your new baby's blood is tested for bilirubin, you'll probably notice a small band-aid on the heel where the blood was drawn. Early treatment for a high level of bilirubin usually involves the use of light (phototherapy). The baby's eyes are covered and he or she is placed under a bright fluorescent light. Most babies who are receiving this treatment can still be brought to their mothers for feeding.

In a small number of cases of excessive jaundice, other treatment such as blood transfusion may be needed. If this is necessary for your baby, your pediatrician will explain what needs to be done and why.

LAUNDRY

New babies can create absolutely amazing amounts of laundry. This is true even if you use disposable diapers. Some babies seem to go through one complete clothing change per feeding.

Your own washer and dryer will make laundry tasks more convenient. If you don't have your own, you'll probably need to buy larger quantities of certain key clothing items. Especially at first, you won't have either the time or the energy to make a daily trip to the laundromat.

Here are some tips to help you deal with laundry.

• Rinse dirty cloth diapers in the toilet bowl right after changing the baby. Flush as you dip the diaper in the water.

• Soak diapers in a small covered pail until you're ready to do a washload of them. A bit of Borax or some mild liquid detergent in the water will help.

• Use a mild soap (if you have soft water) or liquid detergent and the hot water cycle in your machine for baby's wash. The wash cycle need not be long.

61

• Skip the bleach. It may bother baby, and the clothes won't last as long if you bleach heavily.

• Rinse at least twice—three or more times if the water is very hard. It's important not to leave traces of soap or detergent.

• Attack the results of baby spitting up promptly to avoid stains. A solution of baking soda and water may help. "Shout" or a similar stain-removal product may be used. Be sure to rinse thoroughly.

• A dryer is the easiest and quickest way to dry your baby's clothes. It's also expensive. Sunshine does have its benefits in addition to cutting costs. Sun can kill some of the bacteria that tend to hang around on diapers, and it bleaches without leaving an irritating residue. If weather, your location, and your energy permit, you might try hanging the wash out to dry.

At first, you'll do best if you keep your baby's laundry separate from other family wash. After the first several weeks, when your baby's skin is less sensitive, that may no longer be necessary.

LAYETTE

As you read books about infant care or shop for your expected baby, don't be intimidated or even influenced by the long lists of seemingly "essential" items. If you combine all the published lists of infant clothes and then buy the average of the quantities suggested, you'll end up with a lot of things you don't need. (For example, one list which claims to be absolutely basic contains 17 items of infant clothing and bedding that we easily managed to do without for the entire first year.) So our best advice on buying a layette for your baby is don't. See what you get as gifts, and then buy the absolute essentials to get you through the first week or two. By then you'll *really* know what else you need.

Here's a shopping list for getting started. Fill in the numbers you think you'll need.

_____ boxes disposable diapers (get 1 even if you are using cloth diapers)

_____ dozen cloth diapers (1 dozen if you are using disposables, 4–5 if not)

_____ undershirts (you'll go through a lot of these, so get at least 6)

_____ stretch jumpsuits or other sleeping garments

_____ receiving blankets

_____ rubberized sheets to protect cribs (or your lap)

_____ cold-weather garments if necessary (hat, bunting, carriage blanket, sweaters)

_____ bathing and diaper-changing items

(See pages 13–34 for suggestions on what you will need for feeding your new baby. The sections on Clothing [pages 50–51] and Furniture [page 58] will also help you decide what to buy.)

LIGHTING

When you put your baby down, think of his or her position in relation to the lighting fixtures in the room. A light right over the baby's crib makes it easy for you to see the baby. It also could be very uncomfortable for the little one who is lying there looking up at it. Remember that the lights should be located for the baby's comfort, not your ease of viewing.

Be sure that the baby does not have to look directly into a light. New babies don't have the easy ability to change position when they are uncomfortable. So it's up to you to make sure that the light is not located in a way that's bothersome or harmful to your baby's eyes. Note that this caution applies to sunlight as well as artificial lighting! Protect your baby's eyes from strong, direct light.

MOBILES

A newborn baby can distinguish light from dark and can perceive several different colors. Right from the start, a new baby likes to look at faces and other objects, especially those that move. Give your baby interesting things to look at. During the first month, a newborn can focus best on things that are 8 to 10 inches away. Every baby should have a mobile over the crib. You don't have to spend a lot of money. See page 82 for directions on how to make mobiles for your new baby to look at and enjoy.

NAIL CARE

Keep your baby's fingernails and toenails neatly trimmed to help prevent self-inflicted scratches. Cutting a newborn baby's nails is really very easy. Just do it while the baby is sound asleep! Or, if you prefer, you can have someone else hold the baby's fingers while you cut the nails. It's best not to attempt to do the nails of a wide-awake baby without help. Use small, clean scissors, preferably the kind with rounded tips, and be sure to put them safely out of baby's reach when you're done. Some people prefer to use nail clippers, although this would not be our choice for a new baby. Be careful to use either the scissors or clippers very carefully so you don't cut a tiny fingertip.

NAVEL CARE

The stump of your baby's umbilical cord will dry up and drop off. This usually happens within a week or ten days of birth. If painted with triple dye (purple) in the hospital, it will take 10 to 21 days to fall off. The navel may be sensitive for a while after this. Keep it clean and dry with frequent alcohol wipes. Carelessness about this could result in a serious infection for your baby. If any special instructions are required for care of your baby's navel, your pediatrician will tell you what to do.

It's important to keep the navel dry. Cleansing it with rubbing alcohol on sterile cotton (Q-Tips are fine) is the best way. Be sure that the baby's diaper is folded down in front so that it doesn't cover and irritate the navel before this area has healed completely. Do not give your baby a tub bath until after the cord stump has dropped off, the navel has healed, and is no longer weepy (oozing).

NOISE

Most babies can sleep very nicely in the midst of everyday household noise. (Did you happen to notice the noise level in the hospital nursery? People there didn't tiptoe about, or keep their voices in a whisper.) Don't let your baby get used to sleeping in absolute silence. Once you do, you'll find yourself with the burden of keeping it that way. It's easier if your baby can continue to sleep through whatever routine noises go on where you live. This does not mean, however, that you should subject your infant (or yourself) to extreme noises that might cause upset or damage to tiny ears. Noise pollution isn't good for anyone. Use your common sense about noise. Keep your stereo at a moderate level. Don't scream a lot even if you might feel like it. Don't locate your baby right next to a very noisy household appliance. However, it's perfectly all right to go on walking and talking while your baby is resting.

OUTINGS

Fresh air is good for your baby, and you'll probably enjoy getting out of the house too. Use common sense when you dress your baby for going outside. Approximately the same number of layers of clothing you need to keep yourself comfortable will work for your baby. In summer, indoor clothing may be enough. In cold weather several layers might be needed—for example, indoor clothing, a hooded sweater, a bunting, and perhaps a blanket. Be sure your baby's head is kept warm. Babies usually have cool hands and feet, so they aren't a good indication of how appropriately your baby is dressed for cold weather. If the baby's body feels toasty warm, even if the hands and feet are a bit cool, the baby is probably comfortable. A baby who is cold will probably curl up trying to keep warm. Keep your baby out of chilling wind. Winter sunshine is wonderful, as long as it's not shining directly into the baby's face.

When you take the baby out in the summertime, it's best to pick a cool, shady place. Be careful that your baby doesn't get sunburned. A newborn's skin is very sensitive. On a warm summer day, indoor clothing might be enough. If it's very hot, a diaper may be all your baby will need.

It's fine to take even a very young baby for a carriage ride, out to the yard, the park, or other uncrowded places for fresh air. It's best, at first, to stay away from crowded shopping malls, school playgrounds, and any other places where there are lots of people. Your pediatrician will advise you if there's any special reason to postpone taking your baby out for airings.

PACIFIERS (Soothers)

If you decide to use a pacifier to satisfy your baby's sucking needs (see page 70), here are some guidelines to help you avoid the creation of unnecessary problems along the way.

- If your baby is content without the pacifier, don't offer it.

- Make sure you select a pacifier that's safe. It should be *one* piece—that is, the nipple, disk, and handle should be molded at one time of the same material. (Note that the Nuk orthodontic shape pacifier, although claimed by some to be better than others for the baby's bite, is not of one-piece construction. We don't recommend its use.) The disk must be large enough that the baby will be unable to get the entire device into the mouth. Many hospital nurseries use bottle nipples stuffed with cotton. This works for a newborn under constant supervision who doesn't attempt to remove the cotton. Don't try this at home. Your baby could choke.

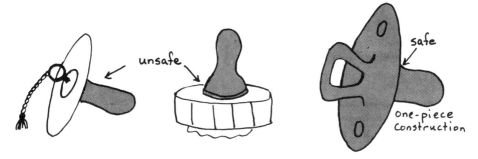

- Never use a string or ribbon to tie a pacifier to your baby or to the crib. Children have been known to choke to death from this practice.

- Don't substitute the pacifier for your attention when what the baby really needs is you.

- Remove the pacifier from the baby's mouth when he or she gets tired and starts to fall asleep. Don't let your baby begin to depend on the device for falling asleep.

- Any time your baby shows signs of rejecting the pacifier cut down on using it.

- Don't use a pacifier beyond the first four to six months. By this time your baby will be using it to satisfy emotional needs other than sucking. It's best not to let this happen.

- Don't dip the pacifier in honey, sugar, or jelly. This practice can get your baby started on a lifetime of dental problems and possible obesity.

PETS

If your household includes pets as well as your new baby, some special precautions are in order for a while. The fleas that irritate your dog or cat aren't good companions for your baby. Don't let the baby share a pet's blanket or toys. Flea collars—on or off an animal—are toxic and should not be within your baby's reach.

No matter how reliable and how much a part of the family your animals are, don't leave your baby alone in a room with them at first. Remember how small and helpless a newborn baby is. The cat that playfully leaps on an infant's face may mean no harm, but lasting fear as well as injury could be the result for your baby. A seemingly gentle dog could turn on a helpless baby with tragic results.

This has been known to happen. Some animals seem to experience jealousy toward a new baby in much the same way as an older sibling might. If you have pets, make sure your baby's bassinet is sturdy enough not to be toppled by an animal. Even if you are sure that your pets wouldn't cause any problems for your baby, there's no point in taking the risk. When your baby is older and stronger, he or she will be better able to meet and enjoy your animal friends. Until then, close supervision is best for all.

POWDERS AND LOTIONS

While powders and lotions are not necessary for care of a baby, many people choose to use them because they feel and smell nice. Most babies enjoy being touched as you apply powder or lotion. Many adults associate the smell of these products with a clean baby.

If you use powder, use it carefully. Don't shake powder directly onto your baby. He or she might inhale some and this can be extremely harmful to tiny respiratory systems. (It's not so good for you either.) Shake the powder into your hand first, and then rub it gently on your baby's skin. Cornstarch is also a satisfactory soother for your baby's bottom and other creases where moisture accumulates.

A bit of lotion may help if your baby tends toward dry skin. You may have gotten samples of baby lotion in your hospital gift pack. Avoid oils for a newborn because they may irritate some babies.

Some pediatricians recommend against the use of any perfumed powder or lotion for a newborn. If your baby's skin seems especially sensitive, you might want to discuss this with the doctor.

SIBLING RIVALRY

The arrival of a new baby can be an exciting and wonderful event in a family. If there are older children, it can also be a source of jealousy and resentment. How should you deal with this? Here are some suggestions.

• Let older children help you prepare for the new baby's arrival. Let them share in shopping, getting the crib or room ready, and helping you pack for the trip to the hospital. Try to make your children a positive part of what's going on. Talk about what it's going to be like to have a new brother or sister.

• Some hospitals permit sibling visits to the nursery. Take advantage of this opportunity if it's available.

• The day you bring your new baby home, go out of your way to pay special attention to your other children. (Think how difficult it must be for a child to sit unnoticed while everyone fusses over the new baby. Make sure this doesn't happen in your family.)

• Plan some time each day to do something personal and special with each one of your other children. This time need not be long, but it must be something appropriate to the child and something each child can count on. For example, when the baby naps you could bake cookies with an older child. If baking cookies isn't your thing, pick something that is. Try reading a story, playing a game, or making something. Have a conversation with your child. Listen to what he or she has to say.

• When an older child sees how much attention a helpless newborn gets, he or she may try acting like a baby too. This is a common occurrence. However, you shouldn't indulge the older child and treat him or her like an infant again. An older child need not return to diapers or be permitted to suck at the breast. Don't reward infantile behavior, but don't punish it either. Ignoring it is generally the best approach. Divert the older child's attention to something else—something appropriate for his or her age. Try calling attention to and reinforcing things which make the older child different from the baby. ("I like the way you put on your own shoes and socks this morning." "Would you and Daddy like to have your orange juice in the new blue mugs this morning?")

• Involve your older children in interesting tasks to help you take care of the new baby, but don't expect them to help you with the drudgery. The new baby should not increase the burdens of other young children in the family. It's better to let the housecleaning go for a while. Don't leave your new baby alone with other young children. It's not fair to anyone or safe for the baby. Even friendly curiosity on the part of an older child could be harmful to a newborn.

• Recognize that some feelings of jealousy are to be expected, and it's important to deal with them. Don't make a big deal about it or feel that you have failed as a parent. If an older child's reaction to the new baby seems unusually hostile—if you seem to be dealing with excessive hate rather than sibling rivalry—ask your doctor for some suggestions. You and your children may need some professional help in sorting out these feelings and dealing with them.

SKIN RASHES

During the first week, many babies develop a rash with little red bumps that look a bit like insect bites. Called "newborn rash," it causes no harm and should be ignored. Time will fade it. Between a month and six weeks of age, some babies develop a face rash that looks somewhat like acne. Like newborn rash, infant acne is best cured by leaving it alone. It should fade within a month. You may notice some white dots on your baby's nose, forehead, or chin. These "whiteheads" are blocked pores, and they will clear up in time. Leave them alone. Resist the temptation to squeeze them. Some babies have reddish-purple spots on the face and neck. These are called "stork bites." They will fade away as time passes.

The above-mentioned skin rashes are best ignored. They take care of themselves with time. Diaper rash and heat rash (prickly heat), however, can be prevented and must be treated if they occur. (See pages 56 and 59.)

SLEEPING

Newborns tend to sleep 16 or more hours out of every 24, although a few seem to manage on considerably less. As you get to know your new baby, you'll probably begin to see a pattern of sleep periods, feedings, and alert awake times begin to develop. At first, the sleep periods may range from about 2 to 3 or 4 hours. As time goes on, one of the sleep periods will probably lengthen. If you're lucky, this sleeping time will occur at night when everyone else wants to sleep. If not, you may have to make some efforts to modify your baby's schedule. A baby who likes to sleep all day and be active all night should be discouraged from taking daytime naps. Wake your baby for daytime feedings even when they are not requested. Try to keep him or her where the action is during the day. At night, on the other hand, you should minimize activity around the baby. Any nighttime feedings should be as brief as possible, and accomplished in subdued light.

What's the best sleeping position for a baby? Most babies sleep comfortably if placed on the stomach with the head turned to one side. Until the baby's navel has healed, however, he or she might do better on the side than on the stomach. These are the safest positions in case the baby spits up while sleeping. If your baby's preferred sleep position is on the back, you'll have to be especially watchful at first. Try to vary your baby's sleeping position, particularly the direction in which you turn the baby's head. A baby who always sleeps the same way may end up with a spot on the head which is temporarily flattened.

If you have the space, it's all right for a baby to sleep in his or her own room right from the start as long as you are close enough to hear the baby whimper. Remember that not all newborns have a lusty cry. If the baby is in another room at night, you'll wake when he or she really needs you, but not for every little sneeze or gurgle. Many parents, however, feel more secure with the baby in their own room for the first few weeks. Whichever you prefer is fine, as long as you are close enough to hear the baby when you are needed.

If you do keep the baby in your room at first, you might be more comfortable if you use a screen to separate the baby's crib from the rest of the room. Although newborns do sleep a lot of the time, some parents find the resumption of their pre-baby sex life easier if they are sure that tiny eyes aren't watching.

SOLID FOODS

Don't be in a rush to add solid foods to your baby's diet. Friends, relatives, and even people you hardly know may pressure you to start your newborn on solid foods. It's best to ignore such advice. Some people mistakenly believe that early introduction of solids will demonstrate their baby to be advanced and superior to infants who still subsist solely on milk.

If you are tempted to push your newborn into consuming the contents of little jars and cereal boxes, here are some points you should consider.

• Nature made mother's milk to be the perfect food for a baby, and commercial formula is the closest possible alternative. During the first few weeks and months, solid foods will not nourish your baby as well as milk will.

• Solids may decrease a baby's interest in sucking. If you are breast-feeding, this, in turn, will decrease your milk supply.

• For the first few months, infants do not digest fully the nutrients in solid foods. Particles of complex carbohydrates, proteins, and fats may pass through your baby without being digested sufficiently to provide the nourishment they should.

• Sensitivity to certain foods is more likely to be a problem within the first six months. A number of babies, for example, cannot tolerate eggs during the first few months but would be well able to handle them at a later date. Some allergies can be avoided altogether by waiting to introduce these foods until the baby's digestive system is more mature and less likely to trigger an allergic reaction.

• Some mothers feel that feeding solids will satisfy a baby and result in longer sleep periods. However, it doesn't always work this way. There's no guarantee that weighing your baby down with cereal will give you a night of uninterrupted sleep.

Your pediatrician will advise you if there are any special reasons to introduce solid foods early to your baby. Four to six months is soon enough in most cases.

SPITTING UP

Spitting up is something almost all babies do some of the time. Some babies do it very frequently. Spitting up is generally a cause for doing laundry, but not a cause for concern. Why do babies spit up? Some babies just consume more than the stomach can hold. In some newborns, the muscle band between the esophagus and stomach just isn't strong enough to keep everything in the stomach where it belongs. So a newborn baby may simply manage to deposit a portion of the last meal all over both of you without any apparent effort. This often happens just when you think everything is settled after a successful feeding. Sometimes you'll wonder how a baby can spit up a quantity that appears larger than what just was consumed, but things often look worse than they really are. Try taking an ounce of milk and splattering it onto your shoulder. See how far it spreads. This little experiment should reassure you that you tend to overestimate the quantity your baby is losing.

If your baby tends to spit up, you'll quickly learn how best to deal with this. More frequent burping helps some babies. Some babies can't stand being handled after feeding. Some do best if held upright for a while after each meal. Do whatever works. You'll find cloth diapers to be handy as protective covers before the spitting and as mops after the fact. (See Vomiting, page 76; Formula Intolerance, page 34; and Nursing Mother's Diet, page 19.)

SUCKING NEEDS

All babies need to suck, and some seem to have much stronger sucking needs than others. While many babies can meet these needs adequately through breast or bottle, a few cannot. What should you do if your baby is one of those who can't seem to satisfy his or her sucking needs at feeding time? Should you offer your baby a pacifier (dummy nipple)? We suggest that you try to avoid this practice if you can.

Before you decide to go the pacifier route, be sure you rule out other causes for the baby's fussiness. (See page 54.) Is the baby hungry or wet? Does he or she have a bubble or other pain? Is attention and cuddling what's really needed? Answer these questions first.

A baby who needs to, will suck on whatever is available, and your baby will probably discover his or her little fists or thumbs soon enough if the sucking need is great between feedings. Hands can't be lost or swallowed. They can be diverted to other uses, while a pacifier often becomes an end in itself. An infant's hands are under his or her independent control and, unlike a pacifier, won't become a crutch in the interaction between mother and baby.

The strong sucking needs of a newborn generally decrease by four to six months of age. Some babies willingly give up a pacifier at this time. Others don't —particularly if the pacifier was used as a continuous device to keep the baby quiet without regard to the baby's real needs at that time.

If you stuff a pacifier in your new baby's mouth whenever he or she fusses, you run the risk of building in a set of responses you'll both be unhappy about later. Toddlers who can't give up the plugs in their mouths are an unattractive sight. A child who becomes dependent on the pacifier to fall asleep may wake up screaming when the device falls out in the night. This will wake you up too.

We recommend against the routine use of pacifiers for most babies. However, we recognize that your baby's particular needs and your tolerance level for fussiness may lead you to try one. Your pediatrician may recommend a pacifier in your case. If you decide to use a pacifier with your new baby, see page 65 for specific suggestions.

SWADDLING

Swaddling (tightly wrapping) your new baby may help him or her to feel secure as well as warm. Some babies seem to sleep more soundly and for longer periods of time if they are swaddled.

Here's one way to wrap your baby securely in a square receiving blanket.

(1) Fold one corner halfway toward the middle. Place the baby's head on that corner.

(2) Bring the opposite corner up over the baby's feet.

(3) Then wrap the other two corners over the baby, one over the other.

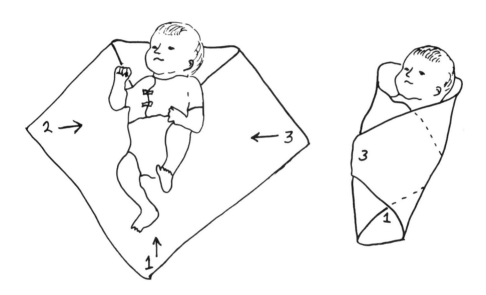

TEMPERATURE (of Baby's Room)

Babies aren't like hothouse flowers, and they shouldn't be kept in overheated rooms or wrapped up in too many layers of clothing. A full-term baby will, if appropriately dressed, do very nicely at whatever temperature you normally keep your home. It's fine to keep your thermostat at 65° F. or even 60° if you wish. Just remember, if you need a sweater to be comfortable, your baby probably does too. But your baby won't need three sweaters if all you require is one. Don't be misled if your baby's hands or feet feel cool. This is normal. As long as the baby's body feels nice and warm, the baby is probably comfortable. A cold baby generally curls up in an effort to keep warm, and will probably fuss. If it's very cold in your home, have your baby wear a little stretch cap (you can make one out of an old stocking) to keep the head warm. (See page 50 for further suggestions on what your baby should wear.)

If you use air conditioning in hot weather, it's fine to keep your baby in an air-conditioned room as long as he or she is dressed appropriately and not located in the direct line of a chilly draft.

TEMPERATURE (Taking Baby's)

There are two ways you can take a newborn's temperature—the rectal method and the axillary (armpit) method. Never put a thermometer in a baby's mouth. You should have a rectal thermometer (that's the one with the thicker, rounded tip) ready to use in case you need it for your baby. A rectal thermometer can be used for both the rectal and the axillary methods. An oral thermometer is fragile. It can be used for the axillary method, but it's best not to use it in a baby's rectum.

Here's how to take your baby's temperature.

(1) Shake the thermometer down so that the mercury is well below the normal mark. This is easy to do. Just hold the thermometer at the high temperature end and snap your wrist sharply a few times. (Don't hold the thermometer over a table or other hard surface while you do this!)

(2) For the rectal method, lubricate the bulb of the thermometer with a dab of Vaseline. Hold the baby face down on your lap and insert the thermometer about an inch into the rectum. If you meet resistance, start again. Do not force. Don't let go of the baby or the thermometer at any time. You can get an accurate reading in about a minute, although 2–3 minutes are better, and you'll be able to cope with holding the baby still for that long even if he or she decides to protest.

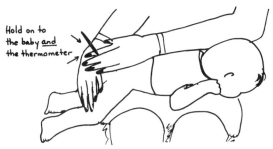

Hold on to the baby _and_ the thermometer

(3) For the axillary method, simply place the thermometer in the baby's armpit and hold the arm to the baby's side. Wait at least four full minutes before reading the temperature.

The rectal method is slightly more accurate than the axillary method. Although some new parents are a bit anxious at first, it's really not very difficult to take a baby's rectal temperature and this method is actually easier and quicker.

One major advantage to the axillary method, however, is that you can use it when your baby is asleep. For a sick infant, some doctors recommend following a rectal reading immediately by an axillary reading. Write down the two numbers for reference and compare them. This will be useful information for the doctor if you later take only an axillary reading as your baby sleeps.

Make sure that you know how to read the thermometer correctly before you need to use it. If you are unsure about this, don't be embarrassed to ask your doctor or a nurse in the hospital. If you need to call your baby's doctor, always report the exact temperature and method you used to get it. Feeling a baby's forehead is not an accurate means of telling if fever is present. You _must_ use a thermometer.

THRUSH

Thrush is a fungus infection which babies sometimes get inside the mouth. This is the same fungus (monilia) which often causes vaginal infections during pregnancy.

Symptoms of thrush are white flaky spots that look like curdled milk. These flakes don't wash off the way milk curds do, however, and the spots may be tender, or painful, and may even bleed.

If you think your baby might have thrush, consult your pediatrician. A prescription may be given for your baby. If you are nursing, be sure to keep your nipples clean, and ask the doctor if medication is recommended for you. Sterilize any rubber nipples or pacifiers that the baby is using.

TOYS

Even newborn babies need things to look at, things to listen to, and things to touch. (See pages 79–87.) Here are some points to keep in mind as you select toys for your new baby.

- Avoid items that might break or come apart. Check for sharp edges and splinters. Remember that whatever it is, it will probably end up in the baby's mouth. Stay away from things with strings. These could choke a baby.

- A toy should be too big to fit into the mouth, but small enough to be held in some way.

- Stuffed toys should be tough. You want the stuffing to stay inside the toy and not end up inside your baby. Stay away from creatures with eyes or decorative features that might come off. Stuffing should be nontoxic and it should have no sharp pieces in it just in case the toy does rip open.

- Bright colors and patterns with sharp contrast appeal to small babies.

- Make sure any paint is nontoxic.

TRAVEL

For long distance travel, flying is usually best if you can afford it. You may spend more money, but you'll save much time and effort. Some families do enjoy train travel, but a long trip with an infant can be tedious. Long trips on a bus are the least satisfactory of all. Here are some hints for handling a newborn traveler.

AIR TRAVEL

The advantage of air travel is that you'll get to your destination with the least time and effort. An infant (under 2 years) pays 10% of the accompanying adult's fare on international flights. Domestic flights are free.

Before You Go

- Make your reservations early. A good travel agent doesn't cost extra, and using one is far easier than calling airlines and trying to figure out the best fares and flights on your own.

- If you have a choice, select a flight that's not at a peak travel time. A less crowded plane means more room for you and the baby, as well as more available help from the flight attendants.

- Nonstop flights or direct flights with only one stop are best. Connecting flights require you to get from one plane to another with perhaps a considerable delay and distance to walk between flights. Of course, you may not have a choice.

- On a widebody or jumbo jet, seats by the doors have the most legroom—more than enough for you to stretch out completely and arrange your baby comfortably en route. (The doors must be clear for takeoff and landing, but in the air the space is yours.) Avoid bulkhead seats in the center, where there may be a movie going on right over your baby's head and a line of people in the aisle on the way to the lavoratories. On standard size planes, seats by a bulkhead or an emergency exit usually have the most legroom. Most airlines will, upon request, reserve seats in advance for a family traveling with an infant. Ask.

At the Airport and On the Plane

- Get to the airport early to check your seat assignment. Most airlines will board you first—or last—so you won't have to stand on line with crowds.

- Some airlines provide a cardboard bassinet that your baby can sleep in. Ask. The basket carrier described on page 47 is ideal for toting a newborn around the airport and on the plane.

- On a full flight, your baby must sit on your lap or be on the floor at your feet. If the plane isn't too crowded, try to get an empty seat next to you.

- If you are fortunate enough to get an empty seat next to you, you can use the seatbelt to secure your baby's car restraint complete with baby. Or you can check the baby's car seat (even unboxed, because it's crash-proof) with your luggage. Remember, you'll need the car restraint to keep your baby safe when you reach your destination.

- Pack a flight bag with everything you'll need en route and then a few extras just in case. You'll need bottles if you're not breast-feeding, one of water even if you are, disposable diapers, and disposable diaper wipes. One change of clothes is a wise precaution.

- Ask the flight attendant where you can change the baby. Some planes have a changing table that folds down from the wall in the lavatory.

- Let your baby suck during takeoff and landing. The swallowing will help keep the ears comfortable as the pressure changes. (That's what the bottle of water is for, in case you prefer not to breast-feed at this time.)

- Especially on international trips, carry at least a two-day supply of formula (unless you are breast-feeding) and disposable diapers with you on board. This will get you through in case your luggage temporarily goes astray.

- Most flight attendants will go out of their way to make you and your baby comfortable. However, the safety and comfort of *all* the passengers is their concern. They are not babysitters.

TRAIN TRAVEL

Long-distance train travel can be manageable with an infant as long as you plan ahead and pack carefully.

• Bring everything you will need to care for your baby en route. You will not be able to purchase any babycare items once you're underway. If you have a lot of luggage with you, pack the things you'll need for diaper changes and feedings in a small bag that's easy to manage with one hand.

• Try to keep your luggage to what you can manage without additional help. Porters are rarely available when you need them.

• Find seats in a car where smoking is not permitted.

• An umbrella stroller will enable you to walk your baby up and down the aisle as needed.

• The lavoratories designed for the handicapped (identified by a wheelchair symbol) are spacious enough for you to wheel the stroller in with you.

• Even if you regularly use cloth diapers, disposables are a must for traveling. Simply wrap up the used ones and toss them into the trash receptacles available in each train car.

BUS TRAVEL

Although usually the least expensive, bus travel for a long distance is the hardest on you and your baby. Avoid it if you can. If you can't, keep these points in mind.

• Bring everything you'll need for the baby. Pack it in a small bag that's easy to handle. Particularly if the bus is crowded, you'll not have any room to maneuver.

• Be prepared to keep your baby on your lap for the entire trip. On a bus, there's really nowhere you can go.

• Practice changing your baby right on your lap. A bus lavoratory is very small and usually unsuitable for tending to an infant.

• Take courage from the fact that the droning noise of the bus will probably keep your baby sleeping for much of the time.

TWINS

About one expectant mother in 80 will be delivered of twins. Sometimes the arrival of twins will have been predicted in advance, but in other cases it will be a surprise. If you do have twins, you'll find that the information in this book pertains to your situation too. Many of the ingredients of good parenting do not vary with the number of children.

The mother of multiples will, however, need to develop strategies for coping with more than one newborn at a time. While your joys may be doubled, your

workload will also be greater than that of a mother with only one infant. You'll probably be very tired. It's toughest at the beginning, so try not to get discouraged. In a few months, your babies will be wonderful companions for each other, and by that time you may even find that two can be easier than one.

An excellent source of information and support for parents of multiples is a **Mothers / Parents of Twins Club (MOTC)**. To find one in your area, check your local telephone book or ask your doctor. You can also write to The National Organization of Mothers of Twins Clubs, Inc., 5402 Amberwood Lane, Rockville, MD 20853.

> If the topic of multiple births interests you, you might wish to read **The Parents' Guide to Raising Twins,** by Elizabeth Friedrich and Cherry Rowland. It was published by St. Martin's Press, New York: 1984.

VOMITING

Spitting up is a normal occurrence among newborns. Vomiting isn't the same as spitting up, and you should be aware of the difference. When a new baby spits up, the milk just gently comes back out and the baby may not even be aware that this has happened. Vomiting, however, is the forceful emptying out of the stomach. The contents are vigorously pushed out of the baby's mouth. Vomiting so forceful that the contents land a foot or more away from the baby's mouth is called "projectile vomiting." This may be a sign of a serious digestive problem or allergy.

Simple spitting up may be a mess, but it's not a health problem. Occasional vomiting if a baby is otherwise healthy is not a cause for concern. However, vomiting that's more often than occasional should be reported to your pediatrician.

ZIPPERS

Zippers and snaps are the safest and easiest fasteners for your baby's garments. Stay away from clothing that ties around the neck in any way. (Later on, of course, you'll use bibs while feeding your baby, but you should never leave anything tied on a sleeping baby's neck.) We've told you this before, but if we didn't say it again here, we wouldn't have the entry for ZIPPERS, which truly makes this an A to Z reference guide!

SECTION FOUR

LEARNING AND ENJOYING

Your Baby's Temperament (Activity, Regularity, Approach–Withdrawal, Adaptability, Threshold of Responsiveness, Intensity, Persistence, Distractibility, Quality of Mood) / Touching (Things for Your Baby to Hold) / How Your Baby Sees / Help Your Baby Look and Learn (Looking at Faces, Colors and Patterns, Looking at Things That Move) / Sounds Your Baby Makes and Hears (Crying, Early Non-Crying Sounds) / Hearing (Babies Can Hear Before Birth, Responding to Sounds, Sounds and Noises, Human Voices, Music for Your Baby) / Books for Your Baby (Which Books Should You Choose?, *Welcome Baby*'s Book List) / Learning and Enjoying

YOUR BABY'S TEMPERAMENT

Right from the start, a baby will show distinctive characteristics of temperament, and it probably won't take you very long to notice that your child has a personal style which influences the way he or she acts. This natural disposition with which your baby was born is likely to set a pattern which will continue substantially unaltered. Try to understand and work *with* your baby's behavioral style, because try as you will, you're unlikely to be able to change it.

Here are some areas of behavior in which babies seem to be born with temperamental differences.*

Activity

Some babies lie very still while you tend to them. Others wriggle about and kick.

Regularity

Some babies seem to be born with a built-in timetable. They eat, sleep, and need to be changed at about the same times each day. A few babies are completely unpredictable, and never seem to repeat the same schedule two days in a row. Most babies are somewhere in between the two extremes.

Approach–Withdrawal, and Adaptability

Some babies don't seem to mind new experiences at all, while others tend to withdraw and shrink away from them. Adaptable babies get used to new things quickly, while nonadaptable children take much longer to adjust to changes.

Threshold of Responsiveness, and Intensity

Some babies are more sensitive to stimuli than others. Some babies respond at the slightest suggestion of a noise, while others may appear to be oblivious to all sorts of surrounding chaos. And when they do respond, some babies respond very vigorously, while others respond with far less intensity.

Persistence, and Distractibility

Some babies cry continuously when they are hungry or in need of attention, and they don't stop until they get what they need. Less persistent babies cry intermittently. Some babies are very distractible, and can be diverted from feeding by anything else going on around them. Other babies seem to be able to nurse without taking notice of anything else.

Quality of Mood

Most babies are generally in good humor. A few babies, however, seem to have been born with a perpetual cloud surrounding them, and nothing seems to suit them.

---

*The material on which this section is based can be found in *Behavioral Individuality in Early Childhood,* by A. Thomas, S. Chess, H. Birch, et al. (New York University Press, New York: 1963).

Babies whose responses tend to be moderate are generally easier to handle. A baby who is especially sensitive, intense, nonadaptable, or difficult to please may be harder to deal with, although such children may be especially exciting and rewarding once you get to understand them. If you understand that certain behaviors are part of a baby's temperament, you will be better able to develop appropriate strategies for dealing with them.

> For further reading on individual differences, and how to handle and enjoy your baby no matter what his or her personal behavioral style, try **Infants and Mothers: Differences in Development,** by T. Berry Brazelton (Dell Publishing, New York: 1986). This book is an excellent resource for helping parents understand the wide range of behaviors that can fall within the "normal" range. Instead of offering rigid prescriptions, Dr. Brazelton's suggestions can help you cope with your baby's individuality.

TOUCHING

Touching—a significant communication system for a newborn who doesn't yet have words—is an essential ingredient of a baby's learning process and personality development. By handling your baby and holding him or her close, you can show your caring. To feel secure, a baby needs to be held and touched lovingly. Babies who aren't held and cuddled do not tend to thrive even if their basic physical needs such as food and shelter are met.

Because holding and touching your baby are such important parts of helping him or her to grow happy as well as healthy, you should always hold your baby in your arms for feedings. Of course, this is taken for granted if you are breast-feeding. If you bottle-feed your newborn, don't prop the bottle and leave the baby. By holding your baby for feedings, you can share the closeness and feelings of warmth and security with your child in much the same way as a mother who breast-feeds.

Don't be afraid to pick your baby up and hold him or her in your arms. It's impossible to spoil a newborn. Babies need to be held.

THINGS FOR BABY TO HOLD

It's important for you to hold and cuddle your baby. It's also important for your baby to have things that he or she can hold. During the first month or two, a baby's little hands are often curled into fists. (For an example of this, look again at the picture on the book's front cover.)

Grasping—holding tight to whatever is placed in the palm of the hand—is a reflex infants are born with. Offer your baby one of your outstretched fingers or a tiny toy, and see how tightly he or she clings to it. By the time a baby is about six weeks of age, the grasping reflex starts to fade, and a baby may not hold on to everything placed in his or her hand. This is not a setback, although it may appear to be. The automatic grasping reflex is replaced by voluntary grasping—that is, the baby is learning to hold on to the things he or she wishes to hold. As this new skill is being learned, some things are going to be dropped along the way.

Encourage your baby to reach for and hold on to things. Provide interesting and safe objects to be held. Small, soft, stuffed toys of different textures are excellent. (See page 73.) Among the interesting objects your baby is likely to find without a lot of help are your nose and hair, your jewelry, buttons, and your glasses.

HOW YOUR BABY SEES*

The once widely held belief that newborn babies do not see much of anything at first is now known to be incorrect. Within minutes of birth, a baby can move the eyes and head to follow an object within his or her visual field. A newborn baby will shut the eyes tightly and keep them that way in the presence of a bright light. At birth, a baby is capable of distinguishing light and dark, and several colors.

Studies of infant vision indicate that objects about 8 inches away are in the area of clearest focus. Anything much farther away or much nearer will be out of focus and will probably appear blurry or fuzzy. For the first month or so, most babies are unable to adjust the eyes to change the area of sharp focus. During the second month, however, a baby begins to develop the ability to accommodate visual targets at varying distances. By the end of three months, a baby's range of visual accommodation (the ability to change the focus from near to far objects and back) is close to that of an adult. Keep this in mind when you have things you want your baby to look at. To be seen clearly during the first few weeks, objects are best located around 8–10 inches from the baby. During the second month, your baby will probably begin to focus well on things at other distances as well.

HELP YOUR BABY LOOK AND LEARN

Looking is a very important part of learning. Approximately two-thirds of the 3 million or so impulses per millisecond processed by the human brain come through visual channels. In an infant, looking, touching, and tasting are closely intertwined aspects of information gathering and learning. Newborns explore with their eyes, their hands, and their mouths.

You can play an active role in furthering your baby's visual development. Here are some general suggestions. The pages that follow contain specific directions for materials and activities to help your baby look and learn.

* Because newborns can't use words to tell you what they are seeing, scientific studies of infant vision generally involve use of sophisticated electronic and photographic devices to measure and record a baby's responses to various visual stimuli.

• Supply interesting things for your baby to look at.

• When you want your new baby to look at something, make sure it's within range of the baby's ability to focus clearly (about 8–10 inches away during the first month). Either bring the object close to the baby, or bring the baby to the object.

• Holding your baby to your shoulder is a good position for seeing things. Most babies become quite alert and attentive when held this way.

• As you carry your baby around, allow time for looking. Stop in front of a picture, the patterned wallpaper, or an object you want the baby to see. Talk about things as you and your baby look at them.

• Enjoy the experience of looking around with your baby. Interest and enthusiasm can be contagious, and if you are visually alert, you are likely to be more sensitive to your baby's visual development.

LOOKING AT FACES

Right from the start, babies like to look at faces. When a baby is nursing, the mother's face is about 8 inches away—exactly in the area of clear focus for a newborn. The breast or bottle is too near to be seen clearly, and it's the mother's face that gets an infant's close visual attention during feedings.

In addition to looking at your face and the faces of other family members or friends, your baby will enjoy looking at simple drawings of faces. Draw, trace, or cut from a magazine a face for your baby to look at. Paste it on cardboard or other backing such as a paper plate. Then tape the face securely to the bars of the baby's crib, or hang it so baby can see it.

The original Raggedy Ann and Raggedy Andy dolls have wonderful faces for your baby to look at. These dolls come in all sizes and are nice and soft for a baby to hold. Make sure the ones you get are well made and safe. Some of the cheap imitations may contain stuffing of questionable safety.

COLORS AND PATTERNS

Babies enjoy looking at patterns. Simple but bold patterns such as checkerboards, bull's-eyes, geometric shapes, and outlines of objects, animals, or faces will hold a baby's attention. Newborns tend to look longer at bold patterns than at solid colors, no matter how bright and appealing the colors may be. So be sure to use colors that contrast with each other to form patterns, rather than one shade at a time. Babies get bored quickly, so make frequent changes in the patterns you provide for your baby to look at.

Here are some suggestions for some interesting things you can give your baby to look at.

• Draw some patterns for your baby to look at. Use bold, dark colors—black, green, red, or blue—so there's lots of contrast. White paper plates make an excellent background, and the resulting product can easily be fastened to the crib or hung where the baby can see it. If you use felt-tip markers to draw the designs, make sure you get the ones with nontoxic ink, in case a design or a marker finds its way to a child's mouth.

- If drawing patterns isn't your thing, cut designs out of magazines and fasten them to paper plates or other firm backing.

- Choose patterned sheets in bright colors for your baby's crib.

LOOKING AT THINGS THAT MOVE

Even a very young baby can move head and eyes to follow things that move slowly within his or her field of vision. Movement attracts a baby's attention, and every baby should have a mobile over the crib. You can, of course, go out and buy a mobile, but here are two simple mobiles you can construct yourself. Because they're inexpensive and easy to make, you can vary them frequently.

Paper Plate Mobile

All you need for this one is a paper plate, cloth tape, and about two dozen small plastic spoons. You'll also need some strong string to hang the finished mobile where your baby can see it. Fasten the spoons around the edge of the plate with the tape. If you wish, you can put an interesting pattern—face or bull's-eye—on the plate where the baby can look up at it. Then hang the mobile.

Coat Hanger Mobile

For another homemade mobile, all you need is a wire coat hanger, assorted small objects to hang from it, and some strong string to hang it all up with. (Clear fishing line is excellent for attaching the individual items and hanging up the entire device.)

Make your mobile using any objects you wish. They should be lightweight, varied in shape and color, and interesting. Here's a picture of one that uses spools, plastic rings from a six-pack of infant formula, colored yarn, small plastic shapes, and a miniature Raggedy Ann doll. Assemble your own collection of things and create a personal mobile for your baby.

Warning: The above suggestions are for making mobiles that your newborn baby can *look* at, not touch. Tie them securely—close enough to be seen clearly, but out of reach. Use lightweight objects, so in case one falls, it won't hurt your baby. When your baby begins to reach for the mobile and there's a chance of success, it's time to move it.

SOUNDS YOUR BABY MAKES AND HEARS

Newborn babies can be noisy little creatures. They cry, nurse and swallow noisily, burp, whimper, hiccup, sigh, grunt, groan, gasp, and breathe loudly. At first these sounds just happen. At birth, a baby does not know how to use sounds to communicate. However, your baby will learn very quickly. Almost immediately, babies find out that crying is a means of getting the attention they require. Crying is a newborn baby's way of summoning assistance.

CRYING

Your baby's cry will be quite distinctive—different from that of any other baby. You may even be able to pick out your own baby's cry in a nursery full of wailing infants. But don't worry if you can't. When you get home, you'll have plenty of opportunity to figure out and respond to your baby's efforts to communicate. (See Crying, page 54.)

EARLY NON-CRYING SOUNDS

Your newborn baby will respond to your voice and your face. Within the first month—sometimes as early as two weeks of age—a baby will begin to "talk" back by saying "ah." Cooing and gurgling sounds will come a bit later—around the middle of the second month. The more you talk to your baby as you feed, change, hold, or play with him or her, the more your baby will "talk" to you.

HEARING

BABIES CAN HEAR BEFORE BIRTH

Even before being born, a baby is able to hear. Your uterus is not a quiet place for your baby to be, and during his or her stay there, your baby will get used to hearing many sounds. The rhythmic beating of your heart, the noises of your digestive system, the sound of your voice and other voices, music, and many other sounds all around you can be heard from within your developing baby's liquid-filled world. During the last months of your pregnancy, you may feel your baby startle when a loud noise occurs near you. Even before birth, some babies seem to be more sensitive than others to certain noises.

RESPONDING TO SOUNDS

How will your newborn baby respond to sounds? Babies tend to respond differently depending on what they are doing at the time. A baby who is awake and alert may move his or her arms, hands, and legs in response to a sound. A sound may cause a baby to blink or to open the eyes especially wide. Sometimes a feeding baby will stop sucking at a particular sound. At other times a baby may suck even harder when a sound is heard.

Sounds—especially your voice—may quiet a crying baby. Continuous whirring noises—an air conditioner or a washing machine, for example—may have a soothing effect on a baby who tends to be fussy.

Even very young babies may make an effort to see where sounds are coming from. They will try to turn to hear a sound, although they may turn in the wrong direction at first. Even very young infants are social beings, and seem to sense that faces and voices go together. Talking to your baby will help him or her to learn this very rapidly.

SOUNDS AND NOISES

While the sound of your voice, or a low-pitched, steady sound may tend to keep your baby calm, a sharp, high-pitched sound such as a siren or a whistle will have the opposite effect at first. Babies usually respond intensely to shrill sounds at first. If you have a whistling tea kettle, try observing your baby when you're boiling water. Some babies will cry at the sound. Others will momentarily appear to be frozen with fear. In the wild, a high-pitched animal cry usually signifies danger and evokes an immediate protective response. Human beings also tend to respond to a shrill cry in this way.

A very loud noise may make your newborn baby startle. If that noise is followed by another and another, the baby may appear to shut it out. This has been demonstrated in studies done in the delivery room. Even at birth, a baby shows the capacity to deal with sounds that may be disturbing.

HUMAN VOICES

Babies like to listen to speech sounds, and they usually attend very carefully to the human voice. Because of this, talking to your baby is very important. Right from the start, you should give your baby as many chances as possible to hear your voice.

The most effective voice tones for quieting a baby and capturing his or her attention are soft and gentle, but with a somewhat higher pitch than a normal speaking voice. While this may place the baby's mother at a slight advantage in maintaining the child's attention and preference for listening, both parents should speak to the baby as much as possible. "Baby talk" isn't required or even to be preferred, although you may, of course, say whatever you wish to your child. Just remember to keep the volume down, the tones soothing, and the pitch a bit high.

Talk to your baby as you perform all the routine tasks of infant care. If you're at a loss for words, try telling your baby what you're doing, step by step. At first, it's not *what* you say, but the sound of your voice that matters most. Before you realize it, however, your baby will be understanding some of what you're saying. When you talk to your baby, remember to call him or her by name, not simply "Baby."

MUSIC FOR YOUR BABY

Babies can listen to and respond in some way to music even before they are born. The regular sounds of the mother's heartbeat are perhaps the earliest influence on the development of a baby's sense of rhythm. A pregnant woman who frequently listens to music is already sharing this music with her baby.

Restful music—rhythmic and gentle and not too loud—can have a calming influence on your baby. Babies love being sung to while they are being held and rocked. Recorded music will do very nicely, but nothing can beat a lullaby sung in a familiar voice. If you do use a radio or recorded music for your baby, don't overdo the volume. Continuous sounds that are very loud (above 85 decibels) can cause damage to tiny ears.

Excellent suggestions for using music with babies from birth to age 2 can be found in **Your Baby Needs Music** by Barbara Cass–Beggs, St. Martin's Press, New York: 1978. This book contains rhymes, songs, and lullabies that even nonmusical parents can master and share with their new baby.

BOOKS FOR YOUR BABY

Right from the start, reading regularly to your baby is a wonderful way to share experiences and promote enjoyment of learning. You needn't wait until your child is walking and talking to begin reading to him or her. There are good reasons to start sooner—when you first bring your baby home, or even in the hospital. Day 1 isn't too soon.

- Infants respond to the sound of the human voice. Having a story to read will give you something to say to your baby even if you're a bit tense or self-conscious about carrying on a one-sided conversation with a newborn.

- Babies like to look at interesting things, especially faces and patterns. The illustrations in some picture books are excellent for showing to your baby. You can easily hold a book within the range of a newborn's ability to focus clearly.

- Setting aside a time for reading each day will build into your family life and routines an activity that will increase in value as time goes on. Your child will derive educational benefits as well as enjoyment from books.

- When you read to your baby, you can hold him or her in your arms. Reading to your baby on a regular basis is a time of sharing and communication both you and your baby will come to count on.

- If you choose the books carefully, reading to your baby will give you a chance to revisit childhood favorites and to find some of the books you might have missed by growing up too soon.

WHICH BOOKS SHOULD YOU CHOOSE?

Here are a few guidelines to keep in mind as you select books for your baby.

- Pick books you enjoy. As you read them to your child, your enthusiasm will show.

- Stories with lots of repetition or rhymes are good to read out loud.

- Select books with pictures that a newborn can look at. Patterns with bold contrasts, and interesting faces will appeal.

- Many excellent children's books are available in paperback, which can save you quite a bit of money. When you find a book you like, ask your local bookseller about the availability of a paperback edition.

WELCOME BABY'S BOOK LIST

You'll probably enjoy making your own list of books for your baby. To help you get started, here are some of the *Welcome Baby* cover child's favorites. (With the exception of *Where Is Willie Worm?* which was not yet available, Ánna Máire was introduced to each of these stories within the first month.)

Goodnight Moon, by Margaret Wise Brown.
Harper & Row, New York: 1947

A delightful story which contains simple text and appealing illustrations. This book can quickly become a bedtime routine. Soon your child will be saying "goodnight" to everything in his or her room.

Babies, by Gyo Fujikawa
Grosset and Dunlap, New York: 1963

An appealing book for and about babies. There are very few words, and the pictures are very dear. The heavy, coated pages (washable) make this a good choice to read during feedings.

Millions of Cats, by Wanda Gag
Coward, McCann and Geoghegan, New York: 1928

A children's classic. The black-and-white illustrations provide bold contrasts and fascinating patterns that will hold a baby's attention. When you read, be sure to hold the book so that your baby can see the pages.

Pat the Bunny, by Dorothy Kunhardt
Western Publishing Co., Racine, Wisconsin: 1962

A hands-on book in which a child can do things such as pat the bunny, touch Daddy's scratchy face, play peek-a-boo, and say "bye-bye." Although it will be a while before your baby can do all these things, this book is fun to have.

The Poky Little Puppy, by Janette Sebring Lowrey
Western Publishing Co., Racine, Wisconsin: 1942, 1970

Babies will enjoy looking at the faces of the poky puppy and his littermates in this Big Golden Book format. The story's lesson will be well worth sharing with your child later on.

The Story of Ferdinand, by Munro Leaf
The Viking Press, New York: 1936

This charming children's story about a bull who prefers sniffing the flowers to fighting in the bullring has stood the test of time. The clear black-and-white illustrations are excellent for capturing a newborn's visual attention.

The Tale of Peter Rabbit, by Beatrix Potter
Frederick Warner and Co., New York: 1903

The lovely illustrations of this children's classic might not have quite enough contrast to suit a very young baby. Nevertheless, we've included this title to remind you just how wonderful a Beatrix Potter story can be.

Where Is Willie Worm?, by **Demi**
Random House, New York: 1981

A simple story with appealing illustrations. A thick, green strand of yarn (Willie Worm) threads its way through the pages, and your baby can hold on as you read.

Ladybug, Ladybug and Other Nursery Rhymes, by **Eloise Wilkin**
Random House, New York: 1979

This beautifully illustrated little book of traditional nursery rhymes has sturdy cardboard pages.

A Baby Sister for Frances, by **Russell Hoban**
Harper & Row, Publishers, New York: 1964

An excellent book to read aloud in your family if you have other children who aren't quite sure they like having a new baby in the house.

The Cat in the Hat, by **Dr. Seuss**
Random House, New York: 1957

A silly story in rhyme, with appealing illustrations. Babies will enjoy the funny faces.

LEARNING AND ENJOYING

Not only is your baby unique, but no two moments with him or her will ever be quite alike. One of the most rewarding aspects of being a parent is the opportunity to share with your child the experiences of learning, growing, and changing from day to day. The suggestions in the pages you have just read were offered with the hope that you would use them as a guide for enjoying your baby and learning with him or her. It's important, however, that you not feel pressured to push your child to achieve. Each baby has a personal pace as well as a personal style of learning. Your baby will grow very quickly, and in looking back, you're likely to be wondering how those days could have passed so fast. Make the most of each one while you can. Provide lots of opportunity, observe and respond carefully to your new baby, and above all, enjoy every moment.

INDEX

To order additional copies of **Welcome Baby** or its companion volume, **Talk & Toddle,** use the order form below. If you plan to have another baby in the future, you might also wish to order **While Waiting,** a guide to the information you need to know about pregnancy and childbirth. Discounts on quantity orders of all books are available to physicians, clinics, or other organizations. For information on prices for orders of 10 or more copies, call St. Martin's Press, Special Sales Dept. Toll Free (800) 221-7945. In New York State, call (212) 674-5151.

Order Form:	Copies	Price
While Waiting: A Prenatal Guidebook ($5.95) (867735)	_____	_____
Welcome Baby: A Guide to the First Six Weeks ($5.95) (861214)	_____	_____
Talk & Toddle: A Commonsense Guide for the First Three Years ($7.95) (784309)	_____	_____
The Parents' Guide to Raising Twins ($15.95) (596618) (See description on page 76.)	_____	_____
Postage and handling: $1.50 for first book and 75¢ for each additional book		_____
Amount enclosed:		_____

Name _____

Address _____

City/State/Zip _____

Send this form with payment to St. Martin's Press/Cash Sales Dept./175 Fifth Avenue/New York, NY 10010. Please allow three weeks for delivery.